CONDOR QATAY

CONDOR QATAY

Anthropology in Performance

Catherine J. Allen
Nathan Garner

The George Washington University

WAVELAND

PRESS, INC.

Prospect Heights, Illinois

For information about this book, write or call:
Waveland Press, Inc.
P.O. Box 400
Prospect Heights, Illinois 60070
847/634-0081

Cover: Based on a design by Veronica Morrison.

Frontispiece: A cross stands on a hill overlooking the city of Cuzco. The cairns at its base include offerings to traditional earth deities.

All text photographs by Catherine Allen unless otherwise noted.

To the memory of
Colin Turnbull

Contents

Acknowledgments

Condor Qatay grew out of years of collaborative work in which many people provided support and encouragement. Our students contributed to our project in many ways; they have been guinea pigs, collaborators, and critics to whom we owe a great deal. We are fortunate that The George Washington University provides a supportive institutional setting for experimental teaching, and that our colleagues in the Departments of Anthropology and Theater and Dance have been both tolerant and interested in our work. The cast and production crew of *Condor Qatay*, as well as our colleagues in theater and dance, threw themselves into making the production of the play a success. Parts of the script and the introduction were published in the American Anthropologist [97(1): 69–82, March 1995]; we thank AA editors Barbara and Dennis Tedlock for their insightful comments and encouragement. Many others provided helpful comments on the manuscript for this book, including Billie Jean Isbell, Bruce Mannheim, and Andras Sandor. We also are fortunate that Waveland Press is willing to provide a home for a kind of ethnographic writing that falls outside the usual academic categories. Our families have supported us with love, patience, and chicken soup through the whole process. To all of these we say, Yusulpayki! Finally, we are grateful to the Andean women and men who provided the inspiration for this play; they are never far from our thoughts.

ORIGINAL CAST

Condor Qatay was first produced by the Department of Theater and Dance of The George Washington University at the Dorothy Betts Marvin Theater on March 31, 1994. The setting was designed by Thora Colot, the lighting by John Blandin, and the costumes by Kristen Kidd. The play was directed by Catherine Allen and Nathan Garner. The cast was as follows:

Marcelina	Melissa Foulger
Vicente	Jonathan Holub
Adriana	Deirdre Butler
Susana	Jen Deitch
José Luis	Ron Johnson
Cipriano and a Hummingbird	Nick Grace
Inocencia and a Frog	Amy Weise
A Condor on Mt. Mallku Tusuna	Jenna Jones
Mestizo Youth/Condor Man	Brian Coleman
A Young Woman	Noel True
Condors who double as the Young Woman's parents	Mark Silver, Kelly Barnett

Introduction

The struggle with words is inherent in any representation of culture. Human events are many-faceted and may be viewed from multiple perspectives. This insight—and the holistic vision it implies—is part of what sets anthropology apart from other social sciences. It is responsible for some of anthropology's special strengths as well as its characteristic problems. One of the most vexing (and interesting) of these problems is the fact that the "totality" of human events is difficult—perhaps impossible—to capture in writing, particularly in the academic discourse of the social sciences. At least since Malinowski's time anthropologists have turned to literary techniques to convey the depth and force of cross-cultural experience as well as the qualitative aspects of culture. About twenty-five years ago Clifford Geertz championed the development of an interpretive anthropology, founded in "thick description." By this he meant ethnographic writing that is both detailed and evocative, writing that communicates culture as a context within which specific actions and artifacts are meaningful. Thick description should help the reader grasp "what people are up to" in the society being described; it should open a window to "the imaginative universe within which their acts are signs" (1973:13).

During field research ethnographers try to participate in a foreign way of life—to shape their behavior in such a way as to make it meaningful and appropriate in terms of the culture they are exploring. Ethnographic writing of the interpretive sort tries to produce a similar, if vicarious, experience in readers by demanding that they extend and exercise their own imaginations in relation to a way of life very different from their own.

The ethnographer practicing "participant-observation" has much in common with an actor, for she or he tries to learn and perform a role appropriate to the social context at hand. In comparing the theater person and the anthropologist, Colin Turnbull wrote,

> as well as observing human behavior we both concern ourselves with behavior that is informative, seeking to perceive consistencies, regularities, patterns, as well as opposites: and then we have to select. We have to select from a mass of data that which is linked together, or can be linked together, to make a coherent whole; and this we have to present in play, ethnography, film or whatever medium we choose, in such a manner as to be comprehensible and (I hope) significant to others. (1979:3)

Condor Qatay grew out of our interest in exploring the common ground between acting and anthropology to see what theater people and anthropologists can learn from each other. We wrote and produced the play as an experiment in anthropology-as-theater and theater-as-anthropology. We wanted to see whether playwriting could provide a vehicle for ethnographic description, interpretation, and even analysis, and we were interested in the ways dramatic performance may communicate ethnographic insights to both audience and actors (see also Schechner 1985).

The play developed through our collaboration at George Washington University where we team-teach a course called "Anthropology in Performance." The course originated in 1976 when Colin Turnbull and Nathan Garner began working together during the mounting of the American production of

The Ik (Higgins and Canan 1984). This play, created by British director Peter Brook and his experimental acting company, is based on Turnbull's *The Mountain People* and additional field notes from Turnbull and Joseph Towles. Garner found that Brook's production of *The Ik* engaged him in a profound way. Even though he was present for rehearsals and had read a great deal about the work, the company, and the Ik before he became an audience member for opening night, his experience that evening was one of being thoroughly captivated. While the fresh theatrical elements of the production caught his interest, his strongest response was stimulated by the subject material itself—the sociocultural world of the Ik. What the production did for him was to make that which was remote and inaccessible both relevant and attainable. In fact the foreignness, the remoteness, the newness, the unexpectedness became compelling theatrical components. Learning about this hitherto unfamiliar society from experiencing the production greatly intensified his connection to the piece.

Since Turnbull and Garner's work together was engendered by this production, it is not surprising that they fell naturally into teaching as they did, developing experiential, performance-oriented course work. Garner's background in Stanislavsky-based acting training—together with some other emotion-based work with which the Brook company had been experimenting, and the use of improvisation in the creation of *The Ik* itself—caused them to base their work with students on getting in touch with the mind-scape of the people rather than focusing on the external trappings of behavior. Furthermore, Garner's intent in developing the course was to broaden the horizons of his acting students; to get them to delve into worlds other than their own and into approaches to character other than simple psychological analysis. Working together, Turnbull and Garner developed a course which uses some reading and discussion, and a great deal of improvisation, to explore cultural worlds rather than individual psyches. The external manifestations of character, the details of individual behavior, develop organically from an understanding or experiencing of the worldview.

Catherine Allen joined the team in 1982, a year before Turnbull left George Washington University. In her fieldwork

Allen focused on how, through the routines of daily life, individual and society are mutually constituted in a dialectical sort of process. Her work centered on the small ceremonies of everyday life and on how these are embedded in the daily routine and intensified in religious ritual. She came to the conclusion that the best way to describe these little ceremonial performances is, very simply, to embody them; the best way to teach about them is to have the prepared student perform them—perform them, that is, not as empty gestures but with the totality of the event in mind.

Since 1982 we—Garner and Allen—have continued to work together. Our course focuses on Quechua-speaking people of the Andes, with whom Allen has done fieldwork. Her ethnography, *The Hold Life Has: Coca and Cultural Identity in an Andean Community* (Smithsonian Institution Press 1988), provides our central text, which the students study rather like a play script. We supplement this with other ethnographic reading as well as with ethnographic fiction, in particular José María Arguedas's *Deep Rivers* (1978). The background reading provides the source material for a number of meditation-like exercises, beginning with some that help the students develop concentration, followed by others that begin to connect students to the Andean land and culture. Included in these exercises is one in which we focus on getting them in touch with an animated, personalized mountain landscape. Using images from the reading material and photographs, each student develops an internal image of an Andean place with which he or she feels a close personal connection. For the rest of the semester students' work is grounded in this relationship to their individual place. From there we begin to set up situation scenarios from the reading, such as waking up, planting, harvesting, chewing coca, etc. These are improvised nonverbally. As the semester progresses, these scenarios gradually begin to cohere until finally the class develops a performance to be presented at the last meeting of the semester.

After a number of years of doing this kind of course, and witnessing the development of a number of very different final performances, we began to succumb to the urge to allow use of the English language. We had always avoided language (other than a few words of Quechua) because of the number of problems its use creates. Students' use of English immediately brings with it their own mannerisms and mental habits, distancing them again from the Andes. Our attempts to solve the problems of using language soon led to the realization that we needed to have a formal script. It is interesting that the play that inspired the collaboration in the first place, *The Ik*, had been developed through many months of improvisation before a formal text was written.

We decided to move from improvisation to a formal script in order to convey, in English, the general style and feeling of Quechua discourse. This necessitated that Allen write all the dialogue, bearing in mind the shape and flow of Quechua dialogue as she wrote down the words in English. She tried to include a certain amount of Quechua vocabulary as naturally as possible—as self-evident exclamations, or words whose meaning she clarifies contextually or through paraphrase. The decision to include Quechua language was made early in the writing process (unlike Icietot, the language of the Ik, which came into that play rather late). Initially Allen was a bit leery of Garner's insistence that she include a liberal dose of Quechua vocabulary and indeed, some of our student actors had quite a struggle with it. Nevertheless, it proved effective in the theater. Once they picked up a few words, the North American audience seemed to feel a sense of co-participation in the action, albeit temporary and vicarious.

Segments of the play were drawn from our situation scenarios, which included coca-chewing etiquette, greetings and partings, divination, and spinning a top. The latter alludes to Arguedas's wonderful chapter ("Zumbayllu") in *Deep Rivers*, in which spinning the top teaches children that rapid movement, light, and sound have powers to open lines of communication with mountain lords, rivers, and distant relatives. In class, we used the *zumbayllu* to introduce some of the ideas involved, more abstractly, in the ritual of blowing over coca leaves (*phukuy*). The top has a similar role in the play. There, a young child, Suzicha, is first seen spinning the top and later begins to spin thread and to chew coca, expressing her transition from child to incipient adulthood.

Condor Qatay attempts to embody as much verisimilitude as possible with respect to the culture of this Andean community, while at the same time incorporating theatrical conventions in a way which renders it accessible (dramatic and engaging) to the contemporary Euro-American audience. We did not want to create a theatrically unconventional, experimental piece—one whose form and conventions might themselves be remote and foreign. We produced it, and intended it to be viewed, almost as if it were ethnographic documentation. Our student actors were all enrolled in our course, "Anthropology in Performance," during the rehearsal period for *Condor Qatay*, in order for them to become immersed in the Andean ethnography. It is this aspect of ethnographic documentation that sets this work apart from most Euro-American theater pieces, be they contemporary, historical, plays in translation, or period plays.

As in *The Ik*, some of the suspense in *Condor Qatay* stems from raising the question: "What new thing am I going to learn next, what is new to me about these people?" In the traditional narrative form of the twentieth-century play, "What new is next?" is a question principally about the events. Other elements such as characters and their relationship usually play a part, but the plot is often the dominant feature. In this work, too, there are character relationships, characters in conflict, and a sequencing of events; however, we want the audience to become as much engaged in the learning process as in these other elements, watching every detail of physical action, every prop, every costume. The detailed playing out of the characters' everyday lives, remote as they may seem, draws an audience closer to the experience of those lives themselves. We have learned that the verisimilitude of the performance can be a richly engaging theatrical device.

In most aspects the play strives to be emphatically realistic. As in any realistic production, the audience must suspend its disbelief to accept platforms and painted drop panels as mountainous terrain, and to accept lighting changes as shifts in time and weather. Ours is a more demanding realism, however, which insists that members of the audience accept much that is foreign to them. For example, we matter-of-factly accept Andean premises about the animate quality of the landscape, and the participation of Sacred Places in human affairs. A less realistic rendering of this idea might use actors to impersonate the Places. However, we chose to have the Places express themselves through the same signs (clearing of the weather, for example) which they would use in the Andes. The most powerful Place, Mount Mallku Tusuna, expresses his reactions to human affairs through the movements of a condor who sits on his peak throughout the play. (This condor, however, is portrayed by an actor dressed in a condor costume; like the setting and light, this is a relatively nonrealistic convention we ask an audience to accept.)

We chose not to include an anthropologist among the characters in *Condor Qatay*. While the play obviously presents Allen's understanding of the rural Andean society she studied, it is not *about* her encounter with that society. Rather, we wanted to create a kind of cross-cultural encounter in the performance, between the audience and play itself, without the presence of a mediating figure. We also wanted to create a representation of these Andean people's lives that would grip the viewer emotionally without losing the complexity of the social and political problems involved. *Condor Qatay* contains no battle cries and pushes no particular social agenda; nevertheless we do not consider the play apolitical or socially uncommitted. Our intent is to engage actors and audience with Andean lives at the grassroots, and to leave them troubled and perplexed by the issues involved.

In *Condor Qatay* we explore the complex and textured fabric of rural Andean society through the microcosm of a single peasant family. While the plot-line resembles a pastoral romance, the environment and society are anything but romantic. The setting—a high, potato-growing community similar to the one where Allen did her fieldwork—is very harsh. All the characters (even the ten-year-old) have endured a great deal of deprivation and grief as their lot in life. As rural Quechua-speaking people, their options are narrow and their well-being precarious; they learn early that people sometimes must be ruthless in order to survive. New opportunities involve high personal and social costs; success is rare. Nevertheless, life is not unmitigatedly grim. Even in these circumstances, resourceful human beings find humor and even beauty in their lives—and we wanted to convey this as well.

The play takes its title and dramatic shape from a widespread Andean folktale about the condor son-in-law, the *Condor Qatay*. A hardy and flexible story like the condor tale continues to be told and retold through the generations because it contains within itself many potential perspectives that speak to the changing present. We wanted in this play to use the condor story to explore the lives and dilemmas of the people Allen knew in the Andean highlands. For example, she drew the character and history of José Luis out of her experience with young men who had attempted to leave the countryside—but who, for one reason or another (bad luck, family problems) had failed to make a go of it. Nevertheless, they had been profoundly changed by their urban experience; rural life seemed unable to provide them with a sense of satisfaction or accomplishment, and they were left with a perpetual sense of disappointment and lost opportunity. Here, we interpret these lives in terms of the condor story as we simultaneously interpret the story in terms of contemporary lives. The play as a whole, by re-presenting this dialectical interpenetration of stories and lived experience, is itself an act of interpretation.

While in rural Andean communities of today one finds a deep connection and continuity with the pre-Columbian past, they are also very different, socially and culturally, from what their pre-Columbian counterparts must have been. Even as we write, these very communities are experiencing a period of rapid, disorienting, and often violent change. Thus, a truthful vision of rural Andean society must express the ways in which continuities exist within the changing present. To a significant extent, cultural continuity is perpetuated through aesthetic preference (taking "aesthetic" in a broad sense)—preferences that affect the way change takes place by guiding individual choices in new and ambiguous situations. The stories people hear and tell are part of this process; they inform the way people understand their own lives and guide, consciously or not, the choices they make. Using the two parallel story lines as we do here comes quite naturally as a way of exploring this issue. In the play the condor story informs the family's life situation, which in turn illuminates the story's significance.

Another theme in the condor story concerns the outsider—the ethnic "other" who must be absorbed into a community and/or kin group; in the process he is transformed and, in a sense, destroyed. Typically, new men are absorbed into rural communities as *forastero qatays*—foreign sons-in-law living uxorilocally (i.e., with the wife's family); after a few generations their natal communities—and sometimes even their original names—are forgotten. (This process has a long history; we find it in the myths of the Huarochirí manuscript recorded around 1600, for example; see Salomon and Urioste 1991.)

On stage, the image of José Luis, the young bulldozer driver in his zippered jacket and sneakers, seated next to Vicente, the elderly Indian farmer in his poncho and chullo, brings home their differences in an immediate, experiential way. However, clothing also is significant in the play at deeper levels and in ways that are quintessentially Andean. As we wrote the script, we found a point of conflict developing around a poncho left by dead José, deceased husband of the widow Adriana. At the end of the play, bulldozer driver José Luis is rather forcibly dressed in this poncho; this felt to us like the right gesture (or code-switch) to express the young man's transformation from *misti* (mestizo) to *runa* (Indian) qatay. At another level, harder to articulate verbally, this gesture shows us a certain truth in a conservative belief championed by Vicente throughout the play: in a sense the dead son-in-law has remained a ghostly presence hanging around the house. José Luis puts on this identity along with the poncho, and henceforth the role will inhabit him as much as he inhabits it.

This brings us to a point that illustrates how much this kind of writing can be, for an anthropologist, a discovery process. We mentioned earlier how putting the poncho on José Luis at the end of the play felt like the right gesture to express his transformation from *misti* to *runa* qatay. It was only after the script was written that Allen noticed while browsing through a Quechua dictionary, that while *qatay* means son-in-law, it can also be used as a verb meaning "to cover with cloth." Apparently the intuitive sort of work involved in the playwriting allowed her to use and explore a connection she knew only subconsciously.

Trapping José Luis. Vicente (Jonathan Holub) stands over his new son-in-law (Ron Johnson) after "covering him with cloth." Suzicha (Jen Deitch) puts the knitted cap on his head as Adriana (Deirdre Butler) and Marcelina (Melissa Foulger) look on. *Photo by Ken Cobb.*

Writing plays or other kinds of fiction gives anthropologists a vehicle—a kind of thought experiment—with which to work out the relationship between the kinds of real people they know and the kinds of situations these people encounter and create in their societies. As in a theater improvisation, they can set a character in a situation and then spin out the consequences in a manner consistent and appropriate to the cultural context. Playwriting (as opposed to writing stories or poetry) provides an immediate check because dramatic performance demands that the vision be embodied and that the script serve as a guide to that embodiment. This forces us to think very concretely, to concentrate (as in fieldwork) on what can be observed—on what people would say and do—not on describing inner thoughts and feelings. Then we can ask, "Does this ring true?" "Would this event happen, and would it happen this way?" "What needs to be changed?" "Does it ring true to our colleagues and to Andean people?"

This kind of discourse is not new. It is inherent in Boas's museum dioramas, for example; but up to now it has existed mainly as an undercurrent at the fringes of anthropology. Although the contemporary "postmodern turn" in anthropology has fostered mainly a critical meta-discourse about the nature of the discipline, it also has allowed this performance-oriented undercurrent to surface openly as a valid aspect of anthropological endeavor (see, for example, Isbell 1995 and Tedlock 1995). The kind of discourse involved is concrete and particularistic, yet probing and open-ended. It exploits the special strength of anthropology to locate the general in the particulars of human life.

We hope *Condor Qatay* will be used in teaching. Besides involving students in the concrete problems of ritual performance and meaning, costuming, music, and so forth, students might try to pick up the story and think about how life might unfold for Adriana and José Luis as a married couple in Chiripata. The teacher might elicit a series of questions—"What will become of José Luis in Chiripata? Could he really set up a small store?" for example—and then explore the kinds of background knowledge needed to actually answer them. The realization that there are no right answers, but rather a spectrum of probability, is an important component of this kind of learning. Students have to confront the way general social processes are played out in particular cases, always taking into account individual character and motivation. Similarly, we hope that *Condor Qatay* may eventually be used and critiqued in an Andean context by the people whose way of life it explores. Here it intersects with the growing use of "socio-dramas" in grassroots development to foster positive dialogue within communities (see, for example, Kleymeyer 1994).

We want to add an observation about what it takes to make this kind of theater piece, and by "make it" we mean to write it, create it in the original, and also remake it or re-produce it. After working on this project, we have become more aware of the fact that the ethnographic accuracy embodied in it is not only a critical theatrical component but also one which is very difficult to achieve. Plays like *Condor Qatay* are hard to write and produce. We cannot envision a theater director deciding to re-produce *Condor Qatay* without first locating an Andeanist anthropologist collaborator. If a body of ethnographic drama is to be produced, it is going to be produced by those who study societies in the way anthropologists do and who also fully understand how a theater piece works and how to make it happen. It will also have to be performed by actors who are committed to cross-cultural exploration and are willing to immerse themselves in ethnographic detail.

While detail is essential to ethnography, a catalog of detail is, as Turnbull commented, "as inherently dull and uninspiring as a snapshot or a static mirror image. There has to be motion and interaction between the viewer and that which is viewed" (1979:2). One way of approaching the problem is to treat the written word as but a transitional phase—a switching point—through which we pass in the translation of lived experience (in the world) to lived experience (as theater), from performance to performance.

CONDOR QATAY

THE CHARACTERS

Marcelina (the grandmother)
Vicente (the grandfather)
Adriana (the mother; widow of José)
Susana, nicknamed Suzicha (daughter of Adriana and José)
José Luis (a bulldozer driver with the road gang)
Cipriano (a middle-aged neighbor)
Inocencia (a neighbor, about Vicente's age)

STORY CHARACTERS

Mestizo Youth/Condor Man
A Young Indian Woman
The Hummingbird
The Frog
Condors
The Young Woman's Family

ACT I

*An Andean landscape—big sky, white mountain peaks in
the distance behind lower rocky hills. It is late in the afternoon. The stage in the foreground consists of raked platforms at different levels. They are all in shadow except the
highest platform, to the upper right, which is a stony mountaintop, Apu Mallku Tusuna. On it sits a large condor slightly
raising and lowering its wings. One of the platforms is the
Story Area where the tale of Condor Qatay, the condor son-
in-law, is dramatized at intervals as it is recounted by old
Grandmother Marcelina. Other platforms are used as a path
(scenes 4 and 10) and a pasture (scenes 6, 7, and 12). On a
lower level is a platform which can accommodate the planting (digging in the dirt) which takes place in scene 8. Somewhat higher up, there is a working stream for scene 3. One
of the platforms needs to be flat enough to double as Inocencia's house in scene 9. Finally, there must be a fireproof
place for the dispachu to burn, also in scene 9. At the lowest
level is a small, rectangular, one-room adobe house, cut-
away to reveal the inside. The door is in the middle of the
long wall on the downstage side. On the opposite wall is a
four-foot-long bench. The stage right end of the house contains a raised bed with storage space beneath it. At the stage
left wall is a q'uncha, a low, clay cooking stove. The walls of
the house have numerous niches which are filled with the
staples of daily life. Over the bed is a corner shelf used for
clothing. There are also roof beams, over and from which
things can be hung.*

SCENE 1

Light comes up on a pasture. Faint sounds of a flock of sheep. Marcelina, an elderly woman, and Suzicha (Susana), her ten-year-old granddaughter, are herding. Marcelina sits on a boulder, spinning with a drop spindle, her woven sling tucked in her waistband. She is looking over the hillside at the sheep. On the ground is a bundle of dark colored cloth. Suzicha is playing with a top on a level area of rock. She sets the top spinning and gazes at it entranced. We hear its hum, faint but insistent. Marcelina turns to look. In the distance the condor spreads his wings.

The top slows, the hum deepens and grows uneven in pitch, then stops suddenly as the top tips over.

MARCELINA: (*stands up*) Suzicha, it's late! (*She tucks the spindle in her waistband and pulls out her sling.*) We should be starting home. Your mother must be cooking by this time. Yau, where's the pig! I told you to watch the pig!

SUZICHA: But that old pig's right down there, Grandma—and the piglets too. We can round them right up on our way home. (*She reluctantly puts the top by the bundle and picks up a stick to use as a switch.*)

MARCELINA: So they are. (*She looks out over the landscape.*) Look, they've done a lot of work on the road today. It's going to go right up Puka Hill, q'inku q'inku, like a snake. (*She traces a zig-zag in the air with her finger.*) Next year maybe we'll have trucks going right through Chiripata!

SUZICHA: They work faster with that new machine.

MARCELINA: What a creature that is! Like a big orange metal—something! Like a—

SUZICHA: Like a snuffly snorty pig, Grandma! —that just shoves along whatever's in its way! They say a new man's come, 'specially to drive it.

MARCELINA: But just look, they've stopped working already. They're finished for the day. They'll be expecting their dinner soon. We should get home and help your mother!

SUZICHA: Grandpa can help . . . (*She longingly picks up her top again.*)

MARCELINA: (*in a sudden flurry; speaking rapidly in a high-pitched voice*) Yau, Suzicha! Those llamas are wandering right into the marsh. Go get them while I bring in the sheep. And no fooling around! Come on, little grandkid—let's get going! Hurry up! Apuriy! Run!

(*Suzicha grabs the top and dashes off, switch in hand. Marcelina quickly ties the bundle on her back and hurries off in a different direction, whirling her sling.*)

SCENE 2

The interior of a one-room adobe house. Adriana, an attractive woman in her late twenties, sits by the q'uncha (low clay stove) stirring a large battered metal pot of soup. Next to the soup pot is a round clay pot full of small potatoes, its mouth covered by a small clay bowl. Vicente, an elderly man, sits on a bench spinning.

The potatoes begin to boil over. Adriana quickly puts down the spoon, pushes the bowl/lid slightly aside with her finger tips and blows into the pot—a delicate but strong gesture. She returns to her stirring.

ADRIANA: Father, can you get me some more salt?

VICENTE: (*looks up but continues to spin*) It's right next to you. (*He nods towards a battered tin can by Adriana's feet.*)

ADRIANA: That's all gone. There's a bag somewhere in the niche behind you.

(*Vicente stands up and pokes around in the niche. A bunch of herbs, ball of yarn, tattered notebook, and half a cabbage come tumbling out.*)

VICENTE: (*only mildly annoyed*) Karahu! Ah, this must be it. (*He peers into a plastic bag, then steps over to refill the tin can from its contents.*)

ADRIANA: Thanks, Taytáy. (*She throws a small handful of the salt into the soup and stirs it. Vicente stuffs the fallen things back into the niche.*)

VICENTE: Why didn't you use this cabbage?

ADRIANA: That's for tomorrow. I can't fix those workers the same old thing every day. Would you just look in that sack for me? I think they brought some noodles. (*Vicente gets up and pulls a sack out from underneath the bench.*)

VICENTE: Here it is. Añañáu! Rice too!

ADRIANA: (*straightforward, without sarcasm*) They don't want to eat potatoes all the time like Indians. They want "civilized food," so they said.

VICENTE: (*with a touch of irony*) Civilized food. Well, at least save out some for us.

ADRIANA: Not much! The foreman will take it out of my salary if he thinks I don't cook it all.

VICENTE: Oh, those mistis won't miss a few noodles. (*He hands her the bag of noodles. Adriana opens it.*) Amayá Wawáy, it's too soon to put them in. They'll turn into mush.

ADRIANA: No, Father, it's not too early—I hear our sheep coming down the hill. (*the sounds of sheep bleating, gradually louder*) Mother and Suzicha are coming back already.

VICENTE: That late already? (*He glances toward the low open door but sits down and continues to spin. Adriana pours noodles into the soup and stirs.*)

(*Suzicha dashes in the door, stops suddenly.*)

SUZICHA: (*folding her hands but speaking breathlessly*) Good evening, Grandfather. Good evening, Mother.

VICENTE: What is it, Hawachalláy?

SUZICHA: (*the words tumbling out*) Grandma can't get the big old machu llama into the corral. She says you've got to go help her!

VICENTE: (*muttering, annoyed; puts down the spindle and stands up*) Karahu! We're too old for this. (*He goes out.*)

(*Suzicha approaches her mother with an air of suppressed delight. As she crouches next to her, Adriana fills a bowl with small potatoes and puts them on the ground between them. Although the two do not touch, their affection is evident.*)

ADRIANA: Here you are, little shepherdess. You must be hungry.

SUZICHA: I am! And I'm cold too! (*She begins to peel a boiled potato with her fingers.*) The old wind was blowing real hard up there in the pasture. (*She stuffs the potato in her mouth.*)

ADRIANA: How's the baby alpaca with the black ears? It looked sick yesterday, and I was afraid the cold wind would be too much for it.

SUZICHA: Grandma was worried about it too. But it seems to be just fine now. And the little piglets are so cute! —running on their little legs! (*She imitates their legs moving with her fingers.*) You should come tomorrow, Mamáy! Grandma can stay and cook for the workers.

ADRIANA: No, urpilláy, it wouldn't be fair. She doesn't like cooking, and it was my idea to take on this job cooking for the road workers.

SUZICHA: But why did you, Mamáy? It seems like a big old bother.

ADRIANA: Well, you just can't get by without money anymore. Here we are, running out of candles and salt and tragu. I can't get more at the Sunday market without money. (*smiles teasingly*) Not to mention that one little shepherdess will be waiting back here for me to bring her sweets!

SUZICHA: Yes, I know, Mamáy. It's just such a bother.

ADRIANA: Yes, money's a bother. It's hard to get money out here . . . not like in town where they all live from money. (*sighs*) Hinayá. That's the way it is.

(*Vicente returns with Marcelina. Both are disheveled and tired from their struggle with the big llama.*)

VICENTE: (*grumbling*) Karahu . . . it's too much for us . . . (*He returns to his seat.*)

MARCELINA: (*wearily putting down her bundle, greeting Adriana*) Mamáy. (*She sits down by the q'uncha.*) That old llama is the devil lately.

(*Adriana hurriedly serves soup into a white enamel soup plate and three heavy brown ceramic bowls. Suzicha carries the enamel soup plate with a large spoon to Vicente.*)

SUZICHA: Mihukuy, Machuláy.

VICENTE: Yusulpayki. (*begins to eat*)

SUZICHA: (*handing one of the ceramic bowls, along with a spoon, to Marcelina*) Mihukuy, Auláy.

MARCELINA: Yusulpayki. (*begins to eat*)

ADRIANA: (*giving a bowl to Suzicha*) You too, Wawacháy!

(*She refills the bowl of boiled potatoes and places it close to Marcelina on the floor; places a woven cloth near Vicente's feet and pours the rest of the potatoes onto it. Then she picks up the remaining bowl of soup for herself. She and Suzicha have no spoons; they drink the soup directly from the bowl, neatly using their fingers to shove chunks of food into their mouths.*)

MARCELINA: You'd better hurry. The road crew stopped working early today. They'll probably be too drunk to eat already by the time you get there.

(*Suzicha puts down her bowl and eagerly begins to spread out her carrying cloth.*)

ADRIANA: (*smiling*) Oh they aren't all that bad, Mamáy. But you're right, we have to go. Come on, Suzicha.

(*Adriana and Suzicha finish their soup. Marcelina helps Adriana put the big soup pot in a carrying cloth and ties it carefully on her back. They make Suzicha a similar bundle with a pile of enamel soup plates. The two duck carefully out the doorway, stooping under their loads.*)

ADRIANA: (*as she leaves*) Haku, Suzicha! Come on.

MARCELINA: (*She begins to peel a boiled potato with her fingers, dropping the peelings into the empty bowl.*) The soup is good. Did you have enough?

VICENTE: Does it matter? She's taken it all with her. (*ironically*) Anyway, we're potato eaters out here. (*He puts down his bowl and starts in on the boiled potatoes.*)

MARCELINA: I don't like her going out to that gang of mistis every evening.

VICENTE: She has Suzicha with her.

MARCELINA: It ought to be you with her! It's too much for her, and it's not safe.

VICENTE: Mamáy, she's not a little girl. She can take care of herself. She's not the first widow to hire out as a cook.

MARCELINA: And she wouldn't be the first one to get in trouble because of it. You ought to go with her!

VICENTE: She's young. Let her do it! I'm getting too old for all this.

MARCELINA: What you're getting is too lazy!

VICENTE: (*vehement, but not angry*) I'm getting too old, Mamáy. And so are you. I didn't think we'd come to this, living here just the two of us with one widowed daughter and a single grandchild. But here we are: our children die and leave us; we stay. I don't know why. But I do know that it's time for us to rest and for younger people to work.

MARCELINA: Seven children . . . and Adriana's the only one left.

VICENTE: Just little Adriana, all alone. And she's the one we didn't think would survive even three years!

MARCELINA: Such a weak little baby . . .

VICENTE: I guess she learned to struggle from the beginning.

MARCELINA: Yet she's alone too. Two of three children gone, and her husband too. Such a strong young man he seemed . . .

VICENTE: Just think, Mamáy, how he was never sick as a boy, not for a single day. When he came to live with us I thought we'd be fine. Who'd have thought he'd start coughing like that?

MARCELINA: (*as if calling him, in the style of a funeral lament*) José, José son-in-law, why did you die? Why did you leave us? Why did you go away?

Your wife is longing for you.

Your little girl is crying for you.

VICENTE: Don't start that, Mamáy. We buried him over five years ago. (*Marcelina inhales as if to continue keening; Vicente leans toward her intently, folds the remaining potatoes in the cloth and hands it to her.*) I'll tell you something, Mamáy. It's high time Adriana brought us another son-in-law. I've been talking with Tayta Melcanor about it, and with the Alcalde and our Comadre Inocencia. There are some good possibilities, boys who wouldn't mind moving in with us, the way José did.

MARCELINA: (*taken aback*) Who?

VICENTE: Well, not here in Chiripata Ayllu, but just over in Misk'i-unu one of Eusevio Lira's sons has just come back from the army. Eusevio has eight children and not enough land and animals to go around. But if this boy marries Adriana he'll get the use of everything we have—all our fields, all our animals. It would be worth it to him to move over here.

MARCELINA: (*musing*) Eusevio Lira . . . And who else?

VICENTE: (*opening his coca bag*) Well, in Yanapata Ayllu, you know how there's that big feud over those fields along the river?

MARCELINA: Oh, they'll never settle that!

VICENTE: Exactly, Mamáy. And they say that Mariano Wanka—the younger one—they call him Wayna Wanka (*laughs*)—is so disgusted with the whole thing that he's ready to leave and try his luck somewhere else. He's not in a position to get much anyway. And he's alone. His wife died last year along with the baby, and her brothers don't help him much.

MARCELINA: (*smiling thoughtfully*) Wayna Wanka . . .Yes, of course. That might be okay. We should talk with Adriana. (*She unfolds her unkhuña, a napkin-sized cloth used for carrying coca.*)

VICENTE: We'll tell Adriana. We've waited too long for her to make up her mind. We know—and she knows—that there won't be another José. That's just the way it is.

MARCELINA: Remember how they played together as children, almost every day? How well they understood each other. José! (*She seems about to lapse back into the lament.*)

VICENTE: (*firmly*) Well, there's nobody like that anymore.

(*He has prepared a coca k'intu and begins doing phukuy—i.e., he has prepared a neat pile of three coca leaves; he blows the k'intu as he waves it in front of his mouth. Light comes up slightly on Apu Mallku Tusuna. The condor raises his wings and cranes his neck in Vicente's direction.*)

VICENTE: Pachamama, Machukuna,
Apu Mallku Tusuna,
Help us speak clearly
to this daughter of ours.

(*He chews the k'intu; prepares one for Marcelina.*)

MARCELINA: (*sighing*) Arí, arí . . . (*blows on her k'intu*)
Santa Tira, Pachamama,
Machula Aulanchis,
Chiripata chikchiqpata . . .

(*She chews her k'intu, then prepares a k'intu for Vicente. They exchange k'intus, and sit quietly for a moment.*)

(*Suzicha, without bundle, comes scampering in the door, followed by Adriana. Both are animated and slightly out of breath. Adriana swings the carrying cloth off her back and unwraps the empty soup pot.*)

SUZICHA: Grandmother! We saw the bulldozer from close up! The driver let me sit on it! (*Her grandparents look alarmed and glance questioningly at Adriana. Suzicha capers around pretending to drive a bulldozer.*)

MARCELINA: Adriana?

ADRIANA: (*laughing*) Oh, it was fine. The machine wasn't running—and the driver is very nice.

SUZICHA: He's a fancy gentleman! He wears gringo shoes, and he has a shiny jacket with one of those zipper things. (*She pantomimes zipping a zipper.*) Zooooop!

Zooooop! (*walks around in circles, continuing to zip and unzip the imaginary zipper*)
ADRIANA: (*laughing*) He liked the soup too. And helped me lift the soup pot—not like most mistis.
SUZICHA: When he was my age he lived in a runa ayllu like this. He told me that while we were sitting on the bulldozer.
MARCELINA: Ah, that explains it then.
ADRIANA: Yes, he speaks Quechua like a real person. Like a runa.
VICENTE: (*who has been only half listening, lost in his own thoughts about a son-in-law*) Sit down and rest, little pigeon, urpicháy. Let's chew coca together and talk.
ADRIANA: Just a minute, Taytáy. I have to fix the dog food. (*She empties the potato peelings into a chipped ceramic pot, adds some water and puts it on the fire.*) There. (*She sits down next to Marcelina, stretches her feet out and begins to open her coca cloth. Looks smilingly toward her father.*) So, how did you like the soup tonight?
VICENTE: (*quietly teasing*) I told you the noodles would get mushy.
ADRIANA: (*laughs, then turns serious*) But what's really on your mind, Taytáy? Something is bothering you. (*Vicente looks at Marcelina.*)
MARCELINA: (*preparing to offer Adriana a k'intu*) Adicha, Wawacháy, you've been a widow for a long time—
ADRIANA: (*abruptly folds up her coca cloth*) Achakáu! I'm forgetting the dogs! (*She jumps to her feet and takes the pot off the fire.*) And I have to check the piglets. (*She leaves quickly.*)

(*Vicente and Marcelina exchange a look of frustration.*)

SUZICHA: (*going to the door and peering out*) It's cold out there, and already dark.

(*Marcelina goes to the door and closes it. She lights a candle which she sets in a wall niche.*)

MARCELINA: (*removing her hat, motioning with her right hand toward Vicente and then Suzicha*) Buenas noches, Taytáy. Buenas noches, Hawacháy.

VICENTE/SUZICHA: (*simultaneously*) Buenas noches, Mamáy.
　　Buenas noches, Hawacháy. / Buenas noches,
　　Machuláy. Buenas noches, Auláy.
VICENTE: It is cold. (*He gets up and sits by the fire.*)
MARCELINA: (*rising and pulling a beautifully patterned poncho
　　off the beam above the bed which serves as a clothes
　　rack*) Here. (*She spreads the poncho, like a blanket,
　　over Vicente's knees.*)
VICENTE: (*looks at the poncho, visibly angered*) Don't give me
　　this one, karahu! (*Marcelina is startled, peers at the
　　poncho.*)
SUZICHA: (*timidly*) That's my father's punchu, Grandmother. It
　　bothers Machuláy.
VICENTE: (*rising, tosses the poncho back on the rack*) What are
　　we doing with that dead man's punchu in our house?
　　We should have burned it with his other clothes—to
　　keep his soul from hanging around. No wonder Adri-
　　ana doesn't remarry.
MARCELINA: José never wore it, Taytáy, you know that. He died
　　before he had the chance. (*relapsing into her mourn-
　　ful reminiscences*) We thought he'd come marching in
　　at Carnival with a big poppy in his montera and his
　　pallay punchu shining . . . but by the time Adriana fin-
　　ished it he was dying. Coughed his heart out. I don't
　　think he ever saw it finished! Ay Taytáy! Achakaláy!
　　The best weaving Adriana ever did.
VICENTE: Quiet! Upallay. All the more reason to burn it.
MARCELINA: I tell you, José never even saw it.
VICENTE: He spun some of the thread, didn't he? He helped her
　　warp the loom, didn't he? They planned it together,
　　didn't they? At least, if you won't burn it, Tayta Cipri-
　　ano could sell it to some gringo in Cuzco. Let the soul
　　follow it to France, or Neuva York—(*sits again by the
　　fire, subsiding wearily*) I don't know, wherever it is
　　they live.
MARCELINA: (*pulls a blanket off the other end of the clothes
　　beam and covers Vicente's knees*) Taytáy, I'll put it
　　away. Here's another one. Let's rest now. Suzicha will
　　be wanting to sleep. (*She sits on the edge of the bed.*)

SUZICHA: Oh, I'm not sleepy, Auláy. (*creeps up on the bed and snuggles up to Marcelina, who pulls a blanket over the little girl*) I get sad thinking about my father. Why don't you tell me a story?

MARCELINA: (*spreading out her coca cloth*) A story, Hawacháy? What story shall I tell you? (*She prepares a k'intu and blows it; sits quietly for a moment. Vicente sits with his legs stretched out by the q'uncha, chewing coca and listening.*) Condor qatay kasqa. The condor who was a son-in-law—that's what I'll tell you about: There was once a man who had plenty of animals—llamas, alpacas, sheep—lots of animals, and a daughter. Now this pretty young girl used to herd his flock for him, every day, way, way up in the high puna pastures.

(*Lights slowly come up on the Story Platform higher and upstage. Dim light remains on Marcelina and Susana. A young woman runs onto the Story Area, sling in hand, looking for a lost sheep.*)

SUZICHA: (*eagerly*) And what happened?

MARCELINA: Well, one day a young man, a misti, came and started following her—that shepherdess, the man's daughter.

(*A well-dressed mestizo youth enters, behind the young woman.*)

SUZICHA: What was he like?

MARCELINA: Añañáu, he was gorgeous, with a white cap and a red neck tie and a fine black jacket—and playing the flute! But—you know something? He wasn't really a young man. He was a condor! A condor who wanted that human girl, that runa's daughter. He just started following her, talking, and playing the flute . . .

(*The young woman is looking away from him as the mestizo pulls out a flute and begins to play. She turns, startled, and is obviously pleasantly surprised and impressed by the elegant young man.*)

MARCELINA: Achakaláy! Poor thing! She could never see him as he really was. She could never see him as a condor.

CONDOR MAN (Mestizo): Yau Phasña! What are you doing?

YOUNG WOMAN: Yau Maqt'a! I'm looking for a white sheep with black ears. I'm afraid it's fallen over a cliff!—And you, what are you doing here?

CONDOR MAN: I'm on my way back to town with a bag full of money I got selling pretty sweaters to Indian girls.

(The young woman is obviously very attracted. Music comes up. They begin to dance an indigenous drum-and-flute waynu. She switches his legs playfully with her sling and he jumps to avoid her. Gradually the sound of a mestizo waynu on brass instruments comes up, growing louder until the drum-and-flute music is overpowered. The condor man holds her hands and leads her in the dance, beginning to take control. Suddenly he transforms back into a condor and flies away with her as the music grows in a crescendo.)

(Music stops and the light fades on the Story Platform as Adriana comes on outside the house with the bulldozer driver in silhouette. He gives her a bundle of plates and they pause, attracted to each other, as he does. They separate, he leaves.)

(Light comes up slightly on the family as Adriana comes in and closes the door behind her, carrying the bundle of metal plates. She is very pleased and excited, but wants to hide this from her parents. She puts the bundle near the q'uncha. Vicente gets up, takes off his punchu and ch'ullu—cap with earflaps—and climbs onto the bed.)

VICENTE: What took you so long? *(He notices the bundle of plates.)* Did you go all the way back for the plates?

ADRIANA: No, Taytáy, don José Luis brought them back, to save me a trip in the morning.

VICENTE AND MARCELINA TOGETHER: Who?

ADRIANA: That nice bulldozer man. His name is José Luis.

(Lights fade.)

SCENE 3

The next day. A spring. A trickle of water flows out of a rock and runs off in a little stream. The early afternoon sky is very blue and clear. José Luis is filling a plastic jug with water. He is an open-faced cholo, about Adriana's age. His demeanor combines a swagger with a kind of naive eagerness. He is wearing sneakers, blue jeans, a tee shirt, and a light synthetic zippered jacket, open; no hat, black hair. When he sees Adriana coming along the path with two ceramic jugs, he hides. She fills her jugs as José Luis watches.

Adriana turns from the stream; she is startled to see José Luis.

JOSÉ LUIS: Buenas tardes, Senoritáy! Are you getting water too?
ADRIANA: Yes, Turáy. I'm getting water for your soup.
JOSÉ LUIS: Ah, qué bien! And I'm getting water for my bulldozer.

(He poses, with one foot on a rock so as to show off his sneakers, and plays casually with his jacket's zipper.)

ADRIANA: *(laughing)* Is it thirsty?
JOSÉ LUIS: Siempre! All the time! For gasoline too. I can hardly
        keep up! *(He smooths back his hair with his hand,
        then bends to flick some dirt off his sneaker.)*
ADRIANA: *(still laughing, but beginning to walk past him, car-
        rying the water jugs)* Well, then you'd better not keep
        it waiting! Allinllaña, Turáy!
JOSÉ LUIS: *(drops his jug and blocks her way; speaks caress-
        ingly)* No te vayas, señorita linda! Quiero quedarme
        contigo, mirando tus ojos . . .
ADRIANA: *(put off and annoyed, yet flattered)* Drunk again?
        Why do men have to drink all the time? How do you
        ever get any work done? *(She tries to walk past him.)*
JOSÉ LUIS: *(amazed and indignant)* Drunk!? I haven't had a
        drop!
ADRIANA: Then talk like a real person!

(José Luis is speechless for a moment, at a loss as he realizes that Adriana dislikes his carefully cultivated mestizo per-

*sona. Adriana walks past him, moving slowly but steadily
with the heavy jugs. José Luis picks up his jug and moves
toward the spring. For a moment it seems that the scene is
over. Then José Luis rouses himself from his daze; he does
not want Adriana to go. He turns to look at her, and puts down
his jug.)*

*(Suddenly he dashes up behind Adriana and, passing her,
tries to grab her flat fringed hat. Thrown off balance, she
drops one of the jugs, which spills. José Luis circles around
her and gallops back to the spring; Adriana whirls around
to face him.)*

JOSÉ LUIS: *(capering and laughing)* Your hat's on crooked!

ADRIANA: *(flustered but pleased; this is a mode of courtship she
understands)* Your head's on crooked! *(She puts
down the other jug, picks up a small stone and
heaves it at him. It barely misses. He pantomimes
great alarm and then picks up the stone.)*

JOSÉ LUIS: Yau P'asña! What an ugly stone! You'll have to find
better ones than this! I only take pretty stones. I like
'em shiny white—and tiny—and round! Like this one!
(He tosses a pebble at her.)

ADRIANA: *(grabs another stone and throws it)* Yau, Maqt'a! How
about this one?

JOSÉ LUIS: Yau! This is big and long! I don't need any more like
that! Hey, take it back! *(He throws it back at her,
barely missing.)*

*(They are circling around each other, giggling. She punches
at his arm and he turns and runs away; she pursues, tossing
a stick at him. Suddenly he wheels around and begins to
chase her, grabbing at the tie strings of her outer skirt.)*

*(Suddenly frightened, Adriana stops abruptly and picks up
the water jug, holding it in front of her as if for protection.
Their wild mood drops away, and they face each other seri-
ously.)*

JOSÉ LUIS: Don't go, Panacháy. I only want to talk to you.

ADRIANA: We can't stay out here like this. People will see us. Anyway, I have to cook the soup or it won't be ready. And your foreman will notice that you haven't come back.

JOSÉ LUIS: You're right. It's getting late.

(He brushes off his sneakers, then regretfully picks up his jug and carries it to the spring; she begins to go off in the other direction. José Luis puts down his jug and turns back again.)

JOSÉ LUIS: *(smiling)* But maybe tomorrow you'll need to get the water earlier—when the sun is about . . . there!

ADRIANA: *(stops and puts down the jugs; laughing)* And will your bulldozer get thirsty earlier too?

JOSÉ LUIS: They only need the bulldozer for a few hours tomorrow, early in the morning. It'll rest all afternoon.

ADRIANA: Then, God willing, maybe we'll meet here again.

JOSÉ LUIS: And if God isn't willing?

ADRIANA: *(Picks up the jugs and begins to leave)* Then we won't.

JOSÉ LUIS: Urpicháy, llama ñawin, don't let me down!

ADRIANA: Sumaqllaña, Turáy! *(As she exits she calls over her shoulder.)* See you tomorrow. Paqarinkama!

JOSÉ LUIS: *(looking after her, playing absent-mindedly with his jacket zipper)* Paqarinkama . . .

(Lights fade.)

SCENE 4

A path, somewhere between Vicente's house and potato fields. Again, late afternoon. As always, a condor is sitting on Apu Mallku Tusuna. Vicente is walking home from his field, laden with a heavy bundle of harvested potatoes. A small, wiry, rather long-nosed man overtakes him. This is Cipriano; he foreshadows the hummingbird of the condor story.

CIPRIANO: *(calling as he catches up with Vicente)* Taytáy! Hamusayki, Vicente Taytáy! Suyamuway! Wait up!

VICENTE: *(stopping and turning)* Taytáy Cipriano, allillanchu? *(He swings the bundle onto the ground.)* I thought you'd gone to Cuzco again. *(He opens his coca bag.)*

CIPRIANO: I missed the truck, it came by early for some reason. So then I had to walk all the way back here. I guess I'll wait and go next week.

VICENTE: Why didn't you take the old high path to Sarachani and catch a truck there? You'd have been in Cuzco before dark. *(They both look up toward the old high path, in the direction of Apu Mallku Tusuna.)*

CIPRIANO: Oh, I don't know, I didn't feel like it. I'll just go next week. All this going back and forth to Cuzco tires me out.

VICENTE: Nobody's making you go to Cuzco.

CIPRIANO: Is that so? When everybody in Chiripata asks me to do their errands? "Compadre Cipriano, bring me some more medicine!" "Cipriano, Taytáy, urpi sunqu, sell these potatoes for me and buy my little boy some sandals!" How can I say no?

VICENTE: Don't say you don't enjoy it. And now everybody in Chiripata owes you favors.

CIPRIANO: Well, it's good to get away from here every once in awhile. And it'll be better once the road is finished. I get so tired of walking between Chiripata and the truck stop in T'ikaloma.

VICENTE: *(blows on his k'intu, smiling)*
Apu Mallku Tusuna,
Path Watcher, Rock Roller.
Condor Tayta, Mallku Tayta
Help us wake up in time
to catch the early trucks!

CIPRIANO: *(laughing)* Yusulpayki, Wayqíy! *(Light comes up slightly on Apu Mallku Tusuna. The condor raises his wings and cranes his neck in Vicente's direction.)* Look, Condor Tayta heard you, that's good. But of course, Mallku Tusuna is your guardian mountain.

VICENTE: *(bemused)* I wonder where that condor's been today . . .

CIPRIANO: You know, over in Quispikanchis they're holding the Yawar Fiesta again. So they say. I heard about it on the truck two weeks ago.

VICENTE: And they snare a condor alive, to play with their little bulls?

CIPRIANO: *(laughs)* Little bulls! Yes, a nice little condor for the nice little bulls.

VICENTE: *(thinking)* Achakáu! To snare a condor! I wonder how they do it!

CIPRIANO: They were talking about that on the truck too. They said there's a misti sorcerer who knows how to do it. He feeds the Mountain Lords the night before and then he goes with his assistant way out in the high plains and sets a trap. Baits it with a dead horse, or something like that. Then he sits for days, blowing his coca leaves and calling the Condor Tayta to come and walk into his snare.

VICENTE: Achakáu! It must fight like crazy! How does he get it back to town?

CIPRIANO: They say he creeps up and grabs it real fast. That's the trickiest part; he has to have an assistant. They wrap a rope around his wings and another around his beak. *(presses his arms to his sides and talks through closed lips)* And then they just carry him home! *(speaking normally)* Later they let him go, if the nice little bull doesn't trample him, of course.

VICENTE: Amayá! Don't even suggest it.

CIPRIANO: *(laughs and turns his gaze in the direction of the new road)* Look, Taytáy, how fast the new road is growing.

VICENTE: *(turning to look)* Next year you'll be able to catch the trucks right here in Chiripata.

CIPRIANO: That new machine makes all the difference. They say the driver knows his job, too. It's only two weeks since he came, and look how far they've gone.

VICENTE: José Luis—naa—what's he called?

CIPRIANO: José Luis Flores Quispe. His father was Hermiliano Flores from Mayumarca, up beyond Wallatambo. I don't know about his mother. There are a lot of Quispes all around there.

VICENTE: Mayumarca! But he's a misti, a city boy!

CIPRIANO: I think his parents moved to Sicuani a long time ago. I don't know for sure but they say his brother-in-law has a store there and makes a lot of money. The wife and I are thinking that maybe he'd be good to have for a compadre. Do you think we should ask him to be godfather to our little Felicha? He could do her First Hair Cutting.

VICENTE: That's not a bad idea.

CIPRIANO: I'd have to do it soon, Taytáy. He's leaving in two weeks. They say he's a good person—he doesn't drink too much and he's well-mannered. What do you think of him?

VICENTE: Me? I've never even seen him.

CIPRIANO: Is that so? *(he pauses)* Odd . . . They say he's always hanging around your house. I thought you'd know him.

VICENTE: *(thunderstruck but deadpan, not wanting to reveal his dismay)* Whose house could that be, Taytalláy? Certainly not mine.

CIPRIANO: It's very odd, then. Not half an hour ago I saw him going into a house and it certainly <u>looked</u> like your house, Taytáy.

VICENTE: *(still trying to seem unconcerned)* Not mine, Taytáy. *(a pause)* Well, *(he looks in a different direction)* what are you going to plant in the Wallaqoto field this year?

CIPRIANO: *(also deadpan, to conceal his amusement)* Maway papa, the little early potatoes. Pretty soon it'll be time to do it.

VICENTE: *(putting away his coca bag)* Well, maybe you'd best be on your way over there now, to check it out. I won't keep you. Go ahead, Cipriano Taytáy, it's getting late. *(He laboriously swings the heavy bundle onto his back.)*

CIPRIANO: Riki, riki, urpicháy. I guess we should be on our ways. *(He shoulders his bundle and they set off in opposite directions.)* Sumaqllaña, Vicente Taytáy!

(Vicente wends his way to his house; a low light catches him as he appears and disappears behind the various platforms, as if on a mountain path. He is hurrying under his heavy load. Shortly before he arrives home he meets Suzicha lugging a big water jug.)

VICENTE: Suzicha! What are you doing?

SUZICHA: I'm getting water for Mama, Machuláy. She couldn't leave because don José Luis is visiting her.

VICENTE: *(muttering)* Hesus María!

(They disappear together as the path goes behind another hillside/platform. Light fades.)

SCENE 5

Light comes up on the house, as in scene 2. Some of the household articles have been stored in different places. Adriana crouches by the q'uncha, peeling potatoes rapidly as she talks with José Luis, who sits on the bench, leaning towards her.

JOSÉ LUIS: I'll peel some of these potatoes for you. Why should I sit here doing nothing?

ADRIANA: Really, you should go. My parents may come home soon.

JOSÉ LUIS: *(looking out the door)* Oh, it's early yet. Why shouldn't I give you a hand? *(coyly)* But if you want me to leave . . . ?

ADRIANA: Urpi sunqu! You know I don't want you to leave! It just makes me nervous when you come into the house. I'm afraid people will talk. *(She searches around the q'uncha for another paring knife.)*

JOSÉ LUIS: Oh, nobody saw me. *(She finds the paring knife and offers it to him.)* I don't need that. Look at this little knife! *(He takes a jackknife out of his pocket and opens it.)*

ADRIANA: Añañau! *(He hands it to her.)* It's beautiful! And folds up in its own little house! What's this for?

JOSÉ LUIS: That's to open cans with. And this one is for bottles.

ADRIANA: It's wonderful! Was it expensive?

JOSÉ LUIS: *(casually)* Oh, not very. I've bought a lot of things with my salary. These shoes, a radio . . . *(as Adriana tries to hand it back)* Go ahead and try it. I'll use yours. *(He picks up the paring knife and begins to peel a potato.)*

ADRIANA: *(teasing)* I didn't know that fancy gentlemen could peel potatoes.

JOSÉ LUIS: I used to help my mother—sitting by the fire in a little house just like this. *(looks around wistfully)* This brings it all back.

ADRIANA: Do you miss Mayumarca sometimes?

JOSÉ LUIS: Well, I miss my mother. I don't really miss Mayumarca. I wouldn't want to live there anymore. *(proudly)* After all, I'm a professional! I don't have to live in a hut like this. When I've saved enough money I'm going to build a big townhouse in Sicuani. *(bends intently toward Adriana and pulls gently on her shawl)* We're going to build it. We'll have a fine wooden floor—not dirt like this—and glass windows with curtains. You'll have a nice kitchen with a big white stove, maybe even running water, a washing machine—everything! Our children will go to the university and study engineering . . .

ADRIANA: *(cutting him off)* No, Turáy! I'm afraid. *(She tosses a peeled potato into the pot, glances at him anxiously as she picks up another potato; otherwise her eyes remain averted.)* What would happen here? What about Suzicha?

JOSÉ LUIS: We can come back for her after a couple of months. She'll be fine here with your parents. *(with growing enthusiasm)* We can bring all three of them back with us! We just have to go ahead and prepare for them!

ADRIANA: *(amused and worried)* Take my father?! I don't think so.

(Sounds of footsteps. Suzicha comes in, very out of breath, with the water jug.)

SUZICHA: *(giving them the water)* Buenas tardes, Wiraqucha. Mother, I'm back. And Machuláy's back too.

(José Luis and Adriana look at each other, startled. Adriana hurriedly hands back the jackknife, which José Luis puts in his pocket. Vicente comes in, calm, courteous and very intense. His face is expressionless but not unpleasant. José Luis stands in confusion. Adriana, looking downwards, takes up the paring knife and peels potatoes all the more rapidly; her face remains averted as Vicente and José Luis converse. Susana crouches by her mother and begins to peel potatoes too, but in a desultory fashion, looking eagerly at the two men.)

VICENTE: *(with courteous formality)* Buenas tardes, Wiraqucha. So you've come to visit me. *(places a folded blanket on the bench and motions toward it)* Please, won't you sit down? TiyaYUUUkuy, Wiraqucha.

JOSÉ LUIS: *(grasping for composure)* Gracias, Señor Vicente. *(sits)* Thanks. Yusulpayki.

VICENTE: *(sits next to him)* Yes, let's just rest and have a little talk. I guess you've been working hard with that machine of yours. *(He opens his coca bag.)*

JOSÉ LUIS: Yes, thank you, Taytáy, let's rest a little.

(Vicente blows a k'intu. Light comes up slightly on Apu Mallku Tusuna. The condor raises his wings and cranes his neck in Vicente's direction.)

VICENTE: Pachamama, Apukuna, Chiripata,
    Let's have a good rest.

(He hands a k'intu to José Luis, and pretends he has just noticed that the young man has no coca bag.)

VICENTE: Ah Wiraqucha, didn't you bring your coca? That's a mistake—you need some, don't you? To share with our Sacred Places here in Chiripata.

(He takes a handful from his coca bag and, rising slightly, offers it to José Luis, who cups his hands together to receive it.)

JOSÉ LUIS: Many thanks, Vicente Taytáy.

(He rather awkwardly holds the coca in his left hand and searches the leaves with his right. There is a tense pause as Vicente watches him prepare a k'intu.)

JOSÉ LUIS: *(blowing his k'intu)*
　　　Pachamama, Chiripata Tirakuna,
　　　Apu Mallku Tusuna . . .
VICENTE: Yes, that's good, Wayqíy. It's Apu Mallku Tusuna who'll be most bothered by your bulldozer. *(Blows a k'intu; the condor shifts its position again.)*
　　　Apu Mallku Tusuna, please
　　　don't be mad, don't be angry
　　　with this nice machine
　　　with the little bulldozer.
　　　It's only here for awhile,
　　　Lord Mallku Tusuna,
　　　it's only here for a few days.
　　　Soon its foul smell,
　　　its ugly noise,
　　　its big earth-biting tooth,
　　　will go far away.

(Adriana stops peeling potatoes for a moment and apprehensively peers at the men from under her fringed hat. José Luis struggles with his mixed feelings.)

JOSÉ LUIS: Yusulpayki, thank you, Taytáy. I wouldn't have known how to say that.
VICENTE: *(beginning to feel expansive and in control)* Suzicha, look in the niche behind you. There's half a bottle of tragu. *(turns back to José Luis)* Let's have a drink, little brother, just a shot or two.
JOSÉ LUIS: Of course, thank you, tomakusunchis.

(Suzicha brings Vicente the bottle and a shot glass and returns to her place. Vicente pours a shot glass of tragu and offers it to José Luis.)

VICENTE: Tomakuy, Wayqíy.

JOSÉ LUIS: Gracias, Taytáy. *(He pours a bit on the floor.)* Pachamama . . . *(to Vicente)* Salud, Taytáy. *(He drinks the shot and hands the glass back to Vicente.)*

VICENTE: *(pouring himself a shot; pours some on the floor and flicks some drops into the air)* Wasitira, Chiripata . . . Mallku Tusuna! Salud, tomanki. *(drinks the shot)* Añañau! Nice an' sweet! *(wipes his mouth with his hand and recorks the bottle)* Now tell me, is this how they drink in Mayumarca, Wayqíy?

JOSÉ LUIS: I think so, but I only lived there until my dad died—when I was about her age *(motions toward Suzicha).*

VICENTE: *(with genuine if grudging sympathy)* Achakaláu! So your daddy died . . .

JOSÉ LUIS: Yes, and there was Mama with seven children. So my sister and I went to work for our compadre in Sicuani.

VICENTE: So young!

JOSÉ LUIS: She helped in the kitchen, and I ran errands and took care of his pigs. But it wasn't bad. He was a good man and raised us almost like his own children. Sent us to school at night— *(proudly)* I finished the eighth grade! *(Adriana stops peeling and glances at him, impressed.)*

VICENTE: *(uncorking the bottle and pouring another shot)* And how did you learn to drive the bulldozer? *(offers the glass to José Luis)* Tomakuy, Wayqíy.

JOSÉ LUIS: Gracias, Vicente Taytáy. Dius pagarasunki. *(drinks and hands back the glass)* Well, first I got a job as a truck driver's assistant. I helped load and unload the cargo and kept track of the passengers. During those years I still went back to Mayumarca sometimes to see my mother. After she died—

VICENTE: His mommy too! Achakaláu!

JOSÉ LUIS: Yes, she's gone now too. I don't go back there anymore. My brothers don't welcome me the way she did. They don't want to share the land with me, and they're jealous of my success. *(brushes his sneakers)* After

all, I might have been just a wakcha, a wandering
orphan boy in Sicuani. Instead I'm a professional, and
they're still out there growing potatoes! *(He realizes
his tactlessness and stops.)*

VICENTE: *(dryly)* And how did you become a "professional,"
Wiraqucha?

JOSÉ LUIS: Well, I couldn't live with my compadre anymore—he
got old and senile, hardly knew who I was—so I joined
the army.

VICENTE: Ah yes, the army! I suffered through that too. *(rubs his
lower back)* I still have pains where the sergeant
kicked me. They beat us when we spoke Quechua, you
see.

JOSÉ LUIS: Yes, us too. Lucky for me that I already knew Spanish. It was hard—but really, I got a lot out of it. They
taught me to drive, and I turned out to be good at it.
Then they taught me to drive the BIG machines, and
that was great! Bulldozers, dump trucks, steam
shovels . . . *(Adriana stops working and listens.)*
When I left the army I could always get work with the
Ministry of Transportation. Now they send me out
wherever they need the bulldozer, and when I'm finished I go back to my sister's in Sicuani.

VICENTE: And during the rainy season when there's no road
work being done?

JOSÉ LUIS: Then I help my sister. She married a Sicuani man
and they have a store. But most of the time there's
work for me on the roads. I earn a salary and *(glances
at Adriana)* I'm saving money. It's a good life.

VICENTE: Is it, Wayqíy?

JOSÉ LUIS: Yes, I love opening up roads with my bulldozer! *(hesitates)* Well, Taytáy, I know the machine stinks and
makes a lot of noise—but we have to make sacrifices
for progress—to bring civilization to the countryside!
(plays with his jacket zipper)

VICENTE: *(dryly)* Yes, Wayqíy, soon we'll eat noodles every day.

JOSÉ LUIS: More than that, Taytáy! Mucho más! Sometimes I
imagine the road opening up before me, like a beautiful snake uncoiling—and I think how it must look to

a bird—or an airplane—flying way up high and watching the roads grow beneath him . . .

(Vicente, nonplussed, reaches for the bottle. As he does so he notices that Susana is looking at her mother in perplexity. His eyes move to Adriana, who is gazing at José Luis in rapt fascination. José Luis looks in the same direction. His eyes meet those of Adriana, and their gaze holds for a moment. Vicente folds his coca bundle and stands up, ostensibly to pour the tragu, standing between José Luis and Adriana as he does so. His former formality and impassivity have returned—he is very distressed.)

VICENTE: *(offering the shot glass to José Luis)* Here, won't you have just one more little glass before you leave, one little glass for your walk back to the bulldozer? *(his voice moves into a higher pitch, and he speaks rapidly in a stylized thank-you)* THANK you, Wiraqucha, for VISITing me, Yusulpayki, urpicháy—

JOSÉ LUIS: *(accepting the shot glass)* Oh, I've finished work for the day . . . *(He notices Vicente's intensity and stops, confused.)* Salud pues! *(quickly drinks the shot)*

VICENTE: *(in the same high-pitched patter)* Oh, my DEAR little Wiraqucha, thank you, THANK you, God will REPAY you for your VISIT. How NICEly you visited me, urpi SUNQU, not even INVITED and yet you just had to VISIT me, how can I THANK you, yuuu-sulPAYKI, urpicháy, WiraquCHÁY . . .

JOSÉ LUIS: *(putting his remaining coca in his pocket and rising awkwardly)* It's I should thank you, Taytáy Vicente, gracias, yusulpayki, gracias, gracias . . . *(He tries to look at Adriana but Vicente is in the way.)*

VICENTE: *(continuing the patter as he impassively herds José Luis towards the door)* And so now you're leaving me, don José LUIS, Wiraqucha, urpicháy, urpi SUNQU, allinllaña, YUU-SUL-PAY-KI.

(José Luis retreats out the door.)

VICENTE: *(muttering)* Get going, karahu!

(He pours himself a shot and gulps it down, then recorks the bottle. Suzicha timidly takes the bottle and puts it back in

the niche, then sits down again. Adriana averts her face. Vicente sits down. There is a tense silence.)

ADRIANA: Suzicha, hand me the tin of salt, won't you? *(Suzicha gets up and brings her the tin. Before she can sit again Vicente speaks.)*

VICENTE: Suzicha, go help your grandmother bring in the sheep. It's getting late.

(Suzicha leaves but hangs around outside the door. Adriana stirs salt into the soup, then puts down the spoon, her face still averted. In what follows, she remains sitting. Abruptly, Vicente goes to Adriana and grabs her violently by the arm. He raises his fist as if to hit her, but stops himself. Adriana shrieks; Suzicha runs back into the house and tries to wedge herself between Vicente and her mother.)

VICENTE: What are you, karahu! Are you a runa woman or are you an animal? Hesus María! Letting him come right into our house! Everybody's talking about you!

ADRIANA: Taytáy! Stop it, Taytáy! He's a good man, you could see that!

VICENTE: I could see he's a misti! He's not a runa, our runa ways aren't good enough for him! Hesus María! Find yourself an ayllu runa, a real husband, karahu! Instead of whoring with the road gang! Karáy! Your mother was right!

ADRIANA: *(frantic)* WHAT!?

VICENTE: *(beginning to regret his outburst)* She said I shouldn't let you go alone to them. That you'd get in trouble.

ADRIANA: Karahu, Taytáy, I'm not in trouble!

VICENTE: Little pigeon, you've been a widow too long. Of course you want a man again, but you need—we need—a regular runa, who can come here as a father to Suzicha—and a qatay, a son-in-law, to your mother and me.

ADRIANA: *(scornfully)* Oh yes, Taytáy, and who might that be? Name me one man around here—who isn't a close kinsman—who isn't mean, or stupid, or sick or old or . . .

VICENTE: *(interrupting)* There's nobody in Chiripata, you're right about that. But just over in Yanapata Ayllu, for example, there's Mariano Wanka, the younger one . . .

ADRIANA: Wayna Wanka! Atakáu! You really must be drunk, Taytáy! Why, they say his wife died to get away from him! He wants to leave Yanapata because nobody there can stand him, why—

VICENTE: Or Eusevio Lira's boy in Misk'i-unu—

ADRIANA: The one just back from the army? Why he's just a kid, and a dumb one at that! What do I want with him? I couldn't stand it, Taytáy.

VICENTE: And I can't stand this, Adriana. You're leading us into poverty. People are laughing at us.

(Marcelina comes in and stops, taken aback. Adriana collapses in tears on Suzicha's shoulder; Vicente turns and picks up his poncho from the bed.)

MARCELINA: *(firmly)* What's going on here? Vicente, where are you going?

VICENTE: *(putting on the poncho)* To find myself a son-in-law!

(He leaves. Lights go down.)

SCENE 6

The pasture. As lights go up, Marcelina is whirling her sling; Susana stands trailing her switch on the ground, staring absent-mindedly into the distance. Inocencia, a small heavy-set woman with a bouncing gait, enters. She foreshadows María Frog of the Condor Qatay story. She is just passing through with a bundle on her back. The three greet each other with pleasure as comadres.

INOCENCIA: Comadre, allillanchu? Wawáy, allillanchu?

MARCELINA: Allillanmi, Comadre Inocencia! Where are you going?

INOCENCIA: *(slowing her pace slightly)* I'm off to the riverside. Take care, Comadre, your pig is rooting near my seed potatoes.

MARCELINA: Don't worry, Comadre, I'm watching her . . . Khuchi! Karahu!

(She throws a rock at the pig—offstage—as Inocencia hurries on her way. Then she sits on the boulder and begins to spin. Suzicha comes over to her.)

SUZICHA: Won't you tell me a story, Grandma? You never finished the one about the condor—what happened after the condor carried the girl away?

MARCELINA: *(putting down her spindle and opening her coca bundle)* What happened when that condor flew off with the runa's daughter? You want to hear about that? Well, I'll tell you. He flew high, high in the air and carried her far away, to his own village . . .

(The lights dim on the pasture and come up on the Story Platform to reveal the village of condors: a rocky hillside; a big nest can be seen between some of the rocks. Several condors are crouching on the rocks, thrusting out their necks and occasionally flapping their wings.)

(The condor man enters with the young woman slung across his back. He swings her to her feet, and she regains her balance looking frightened and upset.)

CONDOR MAN: Here we are! This is my village; these are my people!

(The condors stretch out their necks and stare at the young woman. She gasps and draws back.)

CONDOR MAN: Don't be frightened. They're welcoming you! We're going to celebrate with a big feast!

(The condor man grabs an animal carcass from inside the nest as the other condors descend from the rocks. They form a circle around him in the condor dance. The condor man joins the dance. As they dance they fall on the carcass and rip it to pieces, gobbling it up raw. At the end of the dance

the condor man seizes a hunk for his bride, who shrieks in horror.)

YOUNG WOMAN: But this is raw meat! I can't eat it like this!

CONDOR MAN: It's good, sweetheart! You'll get used to it. *(trying to console her)* Come over here. Let me show you our house!

(He leads her toward the nest. She is horrified and tries to run away, but the condors block her way. As lights go down, the condor man leads the reluctant girl to his nest.)

(Light fades on the Story Platform and comes up on the pasture.)

MARCELINA: *(abruptly folding her coca bundle)* Atakáu! Those lambs are climbing into the ravine! Yau Suzicha! Run after them! Apuriy!

(Suzicha—as if roused from a reverie—runs off and Marcelina calls anxiously after her. Lights go out.)

SCENE 7

We hear the sound of a gentle rain. Lights come up slowly on the pasture, late on a rainy afternoon. A few weeks have passed. Inocencia rushes through, obviously perturbed. She disappears and reappears, wending her way down a mountain path, disappears again.

The sound of rain fades. Lights come up on the house and courtyard. Marcelina is tidying up the courtyard; we see her sweeping the ground with a thorn branch which serves as a broom. Suzicha is sitting on a sheep skin, her hat next to her, pulling burrs out of some newly sheared wool.

We hear a patter of rain returning. Marcelina and Suzicha react, brush raindrops off their faces. Suzicha puts on her hat and continues to work on the wool. Marcelina hurries to finish sweeping.

MARCELINA: The rains are starting early this year.

SUZICHA: I guess they'll have to stop working on the road.

MARCELINA: Well, they're almost done. Some of them have already left. They say the bulldozer's leaving today or tomorrow.

(Vicente enters the courtyard as Marcelina is speaking; he overhears the last remark.)

VICENTE: *(muttering)* And good riddance . . .

MARCELINA: Back already!

VICENTE: I think we're in for some more heavy rain, so I just gathered some firewood and came home. It's back in the corral. Come on, let's get inside.

MARCELINA: *(looking at the sky)* Oh, it's not raining hard—just sputtering a bit. We can stay out a while longer.

(Vicente puts his poncho down near the door and sits on it. Marcelina finishes sweeping, picks up a spindle and sits down next to Vicente, beginning to spin.)

SUZICHA: Maybe we won't use up the wood so fast, now that the road crew is leaving.

MARCELINA: We sure are tired of cooking for them! Even Adriana will be glad to see the last of it.

SUZICHA: She'll miss the money . . .

MARCELINA: But not the work! She really must be sick of it—else we wouldn't be here at home right now while she sits out in the rain with the animals. I didn't really mind when she suggested we change for the day—especially with the hail storm this morning. But I thought she'd take you with her, Suzicháy.

SUZICHA: I've got a cold. Mama didn't want to take me out in the wind.

(Inocencia can be heard as she approaches the courtyard.)

INOCENCIA: Hamusayki!

MARCELINA: Haampu!

(Inocencia enters the courtyard, very agitated. Vicente gets up to help her.)

MARCELINA: Come on, Comadre. Achakaláu, sit down with us and rest!

VICENTE: Sit down, tiyayukuy, Comadre.

INOCENCIA: Comadre, I just chased your pigs out of my seed potatoes. I'd covered them up to keep them dry, and then the next thing I knew your pigs had pulled off the straw . . .

VICENTE AND MARCELINA TOGETHER: *(interrupting)* What! Where was Adriana? Was it really our pigs? / Atakáu! I said Suzicha should have gone too! All those animals are too much for one person!

INOCENCIA: I didn't want to believe it, but I know your pigs, Compadre!

(Cipriano darts into the courtyard, furious.)

CIPRIANO: Hamusayki! Vicente! Your sheep are into my early potatoes. The whole field is ruined!

VICENTE: What! It can't be!

CIPRIANO: They're your sheep, Taytáy! You're going to replant that field for me! All my work spoiled!

VICENTE: Why didn't you tell Adriana? She was herding them today!

CIPRIANO: What Adriana? There was nobody with them. I looked, but there was nobody at all!

INOCENCIA: That's right, I looked too. There's nobody with those animals. They're just wandering loose!

(A moment of stunned silence.)

MARCELINA: Hesus María! Where can she be?

VICENTE: *(frantic)* Maybe she's hurt!

CIPRIANO: *(impatient)* You'd better get your sheep, Taytáy, before they ruin anything else!

VICENTE: *(throwing on his poncho and hat)* I'm going! *(He and Cipriano rush out of the courtyard.)*

MARCELINA: Adicha! My little girl! Where is she?

SUZICHA: *(as the realization dawns on her)* She's gone?

INOCENCIA: *(compassionately)* I'll bring your pigs, Comadre. I shut them in my corral. *(She starts to leave.)*

MARCELINA: I'm coming with you!

(She follows Inocencia off. Suzicha runs to the edge of the courtyard and peers after them. She runs back to the house and peers through the door at her mother's usual place by the q'uncha. She turns back to the courtyard, looking off.)

SUZICHA: Mamáy!

(She runs, bewildered, out of the courtyard. Lights go out.)

SCENE 8

Lights come up on Cipriano's early potato field. Vicente, Marcelina, and Cipriano are replanting the potatoes eaten by the sheep. Vicente does the heavy work with an Andean foot plow (chaki taqlla). Marcelina drops in the seed (which she and Vicente supplied), and Cipriano drops in the fertilizer. The three finish their work, wearily pack up their bundles and leave for their homes, Vicente and Marcelina going off in a different direction from Cipriano.

Light also comes up in the house, revealing Suzicha stirring a ceramic pot of soup. The work crew has left Chiripata, and Suzicha is cooking for her grandparents and herself. The soup has only to cook now; she picks up a spindle and tries to spin, gives up and takes up her top. As it spins on the earthen floor, the top dances into the shaft of light shining through the doorway. Its hum begins to grow—but the soup boils over and as Suzicha reacts the top tips over. Suzicha grabs for the ladle, stirs the soup, blows on it, and lifts the pot to the side of the q'uncha where the heat is less intense. The pot is heavy for her. She looks worn out and unhappy.

Vicente and Marcelina (in that order) enter through the door, tired and muddy. Vicente tosses his hat on the bed; he is both exhausted and disgusted.

VICENTE: Hananáu! We're home. What a day—it seemed endless. *(He drops onto the bench, leans his head back*

against the wall and stretches out his legs.)
Haaa-nanáaaau . . .

SUZICHA: Buenas tardes, Machuláy. Buenas tardes, Auláy.

VICENTE: *(sighing)* Hawáy hawachalláy . . ay Suzicháy . . .

MARCELINA: *(drops her bundle on the floor)* Ay Taytáy taytalláy . . . *(She crouches wearily by the fire, warming herself.)* Hello little cook. How's the soup?

SUZICHA: Fine, I guess.

MARCELINA: It smells fine! Ay, what a day, what a hard day! The wind so cold . . .

VICENTE: . . . the rain just pissing down all afternoon. And nothing to eat but cold ch'uñu. Cipriano didn't bring us lunch.

MARCELINA: *(patiently)* I suppose he thought we should be cooking for him.

VICENTE: . . . all for nothing. All those seed potatoes, our seed potatoes, all that fertilizer, and two of us working all day, for what?

MARCELINA: Oh well, Taytáy, debts have to be paid.

VICENTE: Adriana's debt! She's the one who let the sheep ruin Cipriano's field. She should have replanted it!

MARCELINA: They're our sheep Taytáy. Don't talk like that.

VICENTE: Well that misti made her do it, karahu! He should pay for it! Let him buy the seeds with his salary, let him plow the field with his machine!

SUZICHA: *(who has been ladling the soup into bowls, giggling)* That's too silly, Grandpa!

MARCELINA: It's a bulldozer, not a tractor, Taytáy. Anyway, no tractor could get up that slope.

VICENTE: No tractor, only this tired old Indian! *(fussing, exhausted and furious)* The sneak! The thief! The devil take him! I'll go to the police in Sicuani . . .

MARCELINA: *(amused but impatient)* Oh go on! They'd stick you in jail instead. A tired old Indian complaining to the police! Don't talk nonsense.

VICENTE: I have to do something, Mamáy. I have to do something . . .

SUZICHA: Eat your soup, Grandfather. Then you'll feel better.

VICENTE: I'm too tired. *(Suzicha brings him the soup and tries to give it to him.)* I could throw up, I'm so mad.

MARCELINA: *(taking the soup and handing it to Vicente)* Eat
your soup, Old Man. This is crazy. *(takes another
bowl from Suzicha)* Yusulpayki. And you eat too, little
cook.

SUZICHA: Thanks, Grandma. I will.

*(Vicente grudgingly takes his bowl and starts to eat, then
continues hungrily. As before, Vicente has the enamel bowl
and spoon. Suzicha finishes first.)*

MARCELINA: Don't forget the dog food, little cook. *(Finished, she
gets up and closes the door. Suzicha puts potato
peelings and water in the chipped pot and puts it on
the q'uncha.)* Buenas noches Taytáy, buenas noches
Susana. *(She crosses herself rapidly.)*

VICENTE: *(finished, puts down his bowl and leans his head
against the wall again; wearily)* Mamáy . . .

SUZICHA: *(lighting the candle)* Machuláy, buenas noches.
Auláy, buenas noches.

VICENTE: Where's the tragu? I need a drink.

MARCELINA: *(firmly)* The tragu's all gone.

*(She sits on the floor next to Vicente's bench. Vicente
straightens up enough to open his coca bag. He pulls out
some coca and opens his hand to look at the leaves.)*

VICENTE: I don't understand why my luck's run out like this.
What's the matter with me?

MARCELINA: *(distressed)* Don't talk like that. Enough's enough.

VICENTE: *(blowing on a k'intu in the direction of Apu Mallku
Tusuna, speaks with weary familiarity)* Apu Mallku
Tusuna, what happened to my luck? Why did you let
him take her away?

*(Light comes up slightly on Apu Mallku Tusuna. The condor
raises his wings and cranes his neck in Vicente's direction.)*

VICENTE: *(blowing again)*
Apu Mallku Tusuna,
Old Father, Old Friend,
She was all we had . . . all we had . . .
(He collapses in tears, letting his coca bag slide onto

the floor where Marcelina picks it up.) How could she leave us?

(Again, the condor cranes his neck toward Vicente but seems to lose the connection as Vicente collapses. Lights fade out on Apu Mallku Tusuna.)

MARCELINA: *(trying to keep her composure)* Not <u>all</u>, Taytalláy. Look what a fine little woman our Susana's turned out to be! *(forces a smile toward Suzicha)*

VICENTE: Yes, but it's at least three years before <u>she</u> can bring us a son-in-law—

MARCELINA: *(as Suzicha cringes in dismay)* This little kid! You <u>are</u> crazy!

VICENTE: *(oblivious)* . . . I don't see how we can hold out that long. Who'll plant our fields, who'll pasture our animals, who? who? What if we get sick? What if we get hurt? It's the end of us!

MARCELINA: Stop! *(begins to cry)* Stop! *(puts her hand on his knee; leans toward, but not against, him)*

VICENTE: *(finally venting his grief full-force; beats his chest with his right hand)*
Oh my heart! My heart!
Sunqulláy sunqu!
My heart is bursting!
My heart is breaking!
Oh my heart! My heart!
And my head, my head is spinning!
My head is turning!
Where are you, where can I find you?
Little darling, little pigeon!
How could you leave me?
I looked by the rocks,

(Marcelina begins to lament, see below; Vicente continues his lament)

> I looked by the river.
> I looked on the old high path
> I looked on the new low path.
> I looked all around
> But you were gone.

Ay! my heart, sunqulláy sunqu,
my heart is bursting . . .

MARCELINA: *(drawn into his lament; this is like a controlled explosion of emotion; it should not be too drawn out.)*
Where are you? Adicha Adicháy, Adriana—
Why did you leave us, why did you go away,
My daughter, my sister, my darling, my love?
You were the only one left
How could you go away?
Adicha Adicháy
Why can't we find you now?
Your old father, your old mother,
We're weeping,
we're crying for you.
And your little girl
Your little orphan
What will she do . . .

(Suzicha, miserable, sits silently by the fire. Suddenly she hears Inocencia calling at the door.)

INOCENCIA: *(outside the door)* Hamusayki!

(Greatly relieved, Suzicha runs to the door and opens it.)

SUZICHA: Oh Comadre! It's good that you've come!

(Inocencia comes in. Vicente and Marcelina subside in intensity but continue to cry, and reach for Inocencia as if to draw her into their mourning.)

MARCELINA: Comadre, Comadre, you've come to us—
VICENTE: —to us in our sorrow . . .
INOCENCIA: *(still standing)* What is going on here? It sounds like a funeral!
MARCELINA: My little girl!
INOCENCIA: *(kindly but with authority)* Listen, it's wrong to grieve for the living. You may chase them away, right out of this life.

(Marcelina and Vicente suppress their sobs.)

INOCENCIA: That's right. Your daughter's not dead. *(looks at Suzicha, who is crouching attentively by the fire)* Her mother's not dead. She may still come back to us. They say she's living in Sicuani. Tayta Mario's cousin saw her in the market there.

VICENTE: *(his grief exhausted)* I'm sorry, Comadre. Forgive us. We miss her so much.

MARCELINA: Come sit down. Suzicha, serve our comadre some soup. *(trying to smile)* Suzicha cooked it, you know. Vicente and I were out all day working for Cipriano.

INOCENCIA: *(ignoring the latter remark)* Achacháu! What a little woman! Thanks, I'll have a big bowl!

(Suzicha has been rapidly wiping off the enamel bowl and spoon with a rag. Now she fills the bowl and hands it, with the spoon, to Inocencia.)

SUZICHA: Mihukuy, Comadre.

INOCENCIA: *(accepting the bowl)* Yusulpayki, Mamitáy! *(she eats rapidly)* Aaah, it's fine. Only needs some wakatáy herb. I'll bring you some next time I come over this way.

(As she eats Marcelina and Vicente are composing themselves. Vicente dries his eyes on his sleeve and retrieves his coca bag. Marcelina takes off her hat and brushes strands of hair out of her eyes.)

MARCELINA: That would be nice. Somehow, I never know how to find herbs.

SUZICHA: Oh our comadre doesn't have to find them. She has a little garden by her house.

INOCENCIA: *(smiling, handing the bowl back to Suzicha)* Ah, you noticed. When I find a nice plant growing wild I just ask its pardon and—bring it home! I have oregano, wakatáy, manzanilla, panti panti . . . *(with the slightest touch of mystery)* and some others. They're living in the sunny spot behind my corral, out of the wind. They seem to like it. Even the oregano.

MARCELINA: They'd never grow for me. You know things, Comadre.

VICENTE: *(has been preparing a coca k'intu which he now offers to Inocencia)* Hallpakusunchis, Comadre!

INOCENCIA: Urpicháy! *(blows her k'intu)*
Apu Mallku Tusuna,
Mother Earth and Ancestors,
help your children!

(Light comes up slightly on Apu Mallku Tusuna. The condor cranes his neck toward them. Marcelina and Inocencia open their coca bundles, prepare k'intus and exchange them with each other and with Vicente. Marcelina blows her k'intus but makes no invocation.)

VICENTE: *(wearily, without concentration)* Apukuna, Pachamama . . .

(Suzicha sits next to Inocencia, shyly but resolutely.)

SUZICHA: Comadre, may I ask you something?

INOCENCIA: *(a bit surprised)* Ask away, little cook!

SUZICHA: Comadre, they say you know how to read coca leaves.

INOCENCIA: That's true.

MARCELINA: Suzicha!

INOCENCIA: I don't mind. Now what about it, child?

SUZICHA: Comadre, would you ask the coca leaves whether my mother is well, and whether she'll ever come back to us?

VICENTE: Atakáu! Hesus María! *(to Marcelina)* What's gotten into the child?

MARCELINA: Suzicha! You don't just ask her like that! *(to Inocencia)* Forgive her, Comadre. She doesn't know any better.

INOCENCIA: Isn't she my own little god-daughter? Didn't I carry her into the church? Didn't I hold her in my arms while the priest baptized her? Of course she can ask me, and of course I'll do it!

SUZICHA: *(thrilled and somewhat scared)* Oh, thank you!

VICENTE: *(still embarrassed)* Comadre, we would be grateful. But forgive the request. Right now we don't even have any tragu to give you. Perhaps we can come to you tomorrow evening, with tragu and new coca leaves.

MARCELINA: Well . . . there may be some tragu back in the corner here. Let me check, just in case. *(She gets up and retrieves a bottle of tragu from under some clutter near the stove; hands the bottle to Vicente, who is nonplussed.)*

SUZICHA: *(searches on the bed and finds a plastic bag of coca)* And here's the coca, Grandma. *(hands the bag to her grandmother, who hands it on to Vicente)*

INOCENCIA: I'll be glad to do it right now. Why wait?

(Vicente hesitates, then rises with courteous formality; meanwhile Marcelina spreads dead José's poncho in front of Inocencia, and places a folded unkhuña on it.)

INOCENCIA: Achacháu! *(She picks up a corner of the poncho and examines it.)* What wonderful work! Who made this punchu? I don't believe I've ever seen it.

VICENTE: *(noticing the poncho)* Karahu! Not that punchu again! *(to Inocencia, putting down the coca and tragu)* Comadre, forgive us. We're too upset right now. That punchu's not suitable. Let me put it away.

(Marcelina turns sullenly away.)

INOCENCIA: Now what? This is a fantastic punchu! A real punchu! What's the matter with it?

SUZICHA: Mama made it for my father before he died. Grandpa thinks we should have burned it with his other clothes.

INOCENCIA: For José? Achakaláu! Poor José never got to wear it. *(to Marcelina)* I didn't know Adriana could weave so well.

MARCELINA: *(relaxing a little)* Neither did I. *(laughs a little)* Neither did she. And ever since José died she's had no time. We all have to work so hard.

(Inocencia has been examining the poncho. She turns to Vicente who is still anxious to remove it.)

INOCENCIA: Compadre, forgive me, but this punchu should stay where it is. This is a real punchu. It's waiting for something.

VICENTE: Waiting to be burned.

INOCENCIA: No, not yet. It's not ready for that yet. *(firmly)* Now come, Compadre, let's go ahead and look at the coca leaves.

VICENTE: Hesus María! Well, what can I do . . . *(offering the coca and tragu)* Comadre, Mama Inocencia, forgive this rude request. Please accept this coca and this poor little bit of tragu. Please, Comadre dear, urpicháy, coca knower, coca watcher, find our little Adriana, find out how she is. Find out how we can bring her back. What shall we do? Ask Mama Coca for us, Inocencia, Comadre, urpicháy.

INOCENCIA: *(accepts the coca and tragu; Vicente returns to his seat)* Yusulpayki, Compadre Vicente. I'll ask Mama Coca in your name. *(She puts down the bottle and bundle next to her, unfolds the unkhuña and places it in front of her.)* I need a coin.

(Vicente finds a coin in his coca bag. Suzicha takes it and gives it to Inocencia.)

INOCENCIA: Yusulpayki. *(She puts the coin in the center of the unkhuña; picks up the bottle and holds it toward Vicente.)* Compadre, will you serve the tragu?

(Suzicha takes the tragu and gives it to Vicente. Marcelina finds a shot glass in a niche and gives it to Vicente. She sits down again. Vicente pours a shot of tragu and holds it toward Inocencia.)

VICENTE: Tomakuy, Comadre. *(Suzicha carries the shot to Inocencia.)*

INOCENCIA: Yusulpayki. *(pours a few drops on the floor)* Pachamama, Wasitira. *(flicks a few drops into the air)* Apukuna, Chiripata. *(Then she carefully pours a drop on the four corners and in the center of the unkhuña.)* Tawa iskina. Help us! *(She drinks the bit of tragu remaining in the shot glass.)* Naa!

(She appreciatively wipes her mouth with her hand and gives the glass to Vicente via Suzicha. Vicente pours another shot, which he hands to Marcelina.)

MARCELINA: Yusulpayki. *(She does a libation and flicks drops into the air.)* Salud. *(drinks the shot and hands the glass back to Vicente)*

VICENTE: *(pours himself a shot, pours a libation on the ground)* Pachamama . . . *(flicks drops into the air)* Apukuna, Mallku Tusuna . . . Salud. *(drinks the shot; pours another glass for Inocencia)*

INOCENCIA: *(accepting the shot glass)* Salud. Tomakusunchis.

(She drinks the shot and hands back the glass via Suzicha. Vicente corks the bottle, then crouches next to Inocencia. Inocencia opens the plastic bag of coca, and transfers a large handful from the bag to her own unkhuña. Then she takes a handful in her left hand, and blows over it.)

INOCENCIA: Coca Mama, Pacha Mama,
Apu Mallku Tusuna,
Hills of Chiripata,
Hills of Sicuani,
tell us clearly
about our daughter,
about Adriana,
a Chiripata runa's daughter
who's gone away.
TELL US CLEARLY!

(She opens her hand and lets the leaves fall onto the open unkhuña over the coin in the center. Light comes up strongly on Apu Mallku Tusuna. The condor raises its wings and intensifies its stretch towards the family. Inocencia studies the leaves very intently. The other three look anxiously at the leaves, glancing occasionally at Inocencia. Inocencia points to a leaf near the edge of the cloth whose tip points toward the center.)

INOCENCIA: Look! This is Adriana. And this one is José Luis. These in the center—see, two big leaves and one little one—these are the three of you. *(She pauses again, studying the leaves intently.)* Adriana is turning back toward her home, away from José Luis. Their luck is not going well. They are poor. I see a loss. . . . Here it is. *(She points to a crumpled leaf that fell out-*

side the unkhuña.) Gone for good. Aah . . . *(pauses again, then looks sadly at Marcelina)* . . . and other misfortune. *(She points to another crumpled leaf.)*

SUZICHA: What happened? Is Mama all right?

INOCENCIA: *(puts her hand comfortingly on Suzicha's head)* Adriana's heart is longing for Suzicha . . . and for Chiripata. Maybe the Apu is drawing her back. But look . . . here . . . José Luis's leaf is attached to hers. He won't want to let her go . . . *(pauses intently, as if listening)*. . . and . . . that's all. That's all I can tell you.

(Light goes down on Apu Mallku Tusuna as Inocencia sags wearily and folds the unkhuña. The others relax along with her. All are tired out from the mental exertion. Vicente returns to his seat and uncorks the bottle.)

INOCENCIA: Haa-nanáu . . .

VICENTE: *(pouring a shot)* Many thanks, Comadre. Tomakuy.

INOCENCIA: Yusulpayki. Salud! *(drinks and hands back the glass)*

SUZICHA: She's coming back! Did you say that she's coming back?

MARCELINA: Comadre, how can we hold her heart and bring her home to Chiripata?

INOCENCIA: Apu Mallku Tusuna will help you. He's sad too, and wants Adriana back. But you must feed him and ask for his help. You should offer him a dispachu, a medicine bundle.

VICENTE: Let's prepare it now! I think we have the ingredients.

INOCENCIA: Not now, Compadre. Your thoughts aren't steady enough tonight. You're too tired, and too upset. Come to my house tomorrow evening—no, tomorrow's Friday, manan allinchu, Friday's no good for making medicine—come day after tomorrow, in the evening, and I'll help you. And rest, if you can, between now and then. Eat well—but go easy on the hot pepper!

VICENTE: What hot pepper? We haven't got any . . .

INOCENCIA: No salt either, Compadre. Bring coca and tragu when you come. I'll get the medicine for you, but you must place it in the offering with your own hand.

VICENTE: Good. I'll do that, Comadre.

INOCENCIA: Keep in mind, Vicente, that if Adriana comes back here, José Luis will follow her.

VICENTE: Just let him try! Karahu! I'll have a nice collection of stones waiting to throw at him! And a pack of dogs to run him right out of Chiripata!

INOCENCIA: Steady yourself, Compadre. You're not thinking. Now listen to me. José Luis has his problems in town. He's poor and he's in some kind of trouble. He loves Adriana.

MARCELINA: *(thoughtfully)* Then, if that's true . . .

INOCENCIA: Of course it's true! Didn't the coca say so?

VICENTE: What do I care about his troubles! I just want to keep him away from here!

INOCENCIA: Achakaláu! Compadre, is your head on backwards? Don't you need someone here? A young man, someone to help you in your old age?

MARCELINA: It's all he thinks about.

VICENTE: *(startled, then annoyed)* You don't mean—?

INOCENCIA: I mean you have to think, Compadre, about how to snare yourself a son-in-law.

VICENTE: I have to think about a runa son-in-law, a real person like us, who wants to live our way of life. What do I want with this misti, this city boy with his smelly machines and fancy airs?

INOCENCIA: José Luis comes from Mayumarca, a runa ayllu like Chiripata. His parents were Indians, like us. He speaks our language. People here liked him. I think he could live here if he had to.

VICENTE: But he doesn't have to. And he doesn't want to. He's on to better things— *(bitterly sarcastic)* progress! civilization!

INOCENCIA: Well, I can only tell you what the coca said, Compadre. José Luis is having a hard time in the city, and he loves Adriana. Think about it. This may be your chance, if you can see it clearly. *(She stands up.)* And now, I should go. It'll be a long steep walk to my house.

(She begins to gather up her bundle. Meanwhile, the night outside the house has been brightening.)

MARCELINA: We'll go with you Comadre! You shouldn't have to walk home alone in the dark.

VICENTE: Of course, we'll all go together. *(muttering to himself as he lights a small tin lantern)* Snare a son-in-law . . .

MARCELINA: And here, Comadre, take your tragu. *(She puts the tragu in Inocencia's bundle.)*

VICENTE: Suzicha, go look for the dogs. We'll take them with us.

SUZICHA: *(excited and happy)* Of course, Grandpa. Oh, and I mustn't forget to feed them either!

MARCELINA: That can wait until we get back.

(Suzicha runs out the door. She stops in surprise as she sees how the weather has cleared and the mountains are shining in the moonlight. She runs back in.)

SUZICHA: It's not raining anymore and the moon's shining! We won't even need the lantern!

MARCELINA: Ah, Mother Moon! That's good!

(Suzicha goes back out and runs behind the house looking for the dogs. Inocencia swings the bundle onto her back. Vicente puts on his poncho and hat; Marcelina wraps up in her shawl and puts on her montera. They go outside. Marcelina closes the door carefully behind them.)

INOCENCIA: Mama Killa! Bright as day!

VICENTE: *(blowing out the lantern)* Suzicha was right. We won't need the lantern.

MARCELINA: Bring it along just in case! *(She takes it from Vicente.)*

(Light grows more intense on Apu Mallku Tusuna. The condor spreads its wings, which glitter in the moonlight. Vicente prepares a k'intu.)

VICENTE: *(blowing the k'intu)*
Apu Mallku Tusuna!
Star Father! Snow Father!

INOCENCIA: Come on, let's go, Compadre, while the weather holds.

MARCELINA: Suzicha! Wait for us!

(They start off. Light fades on the house and courtyard, but remains shining intensely on Apu Mallku Tusuna. The condor cranes its neck and spreads its wings. Music comes up as light fades.)

ACT II

SCENE 9

Evening two days later. Two areas are lit: 1) The interior of Inocencia's house—only the q'uncha is visible, lighting a small area of the floor. Inocencia is seated on the floor, studying some dispachu ingredients and a piece of white paper spread out on a cloth in front of her. 2) Marcelina and Suzicha are at home, sitting next to their q'uncha. Marcelina is chewing coca. Suzicha is playing with her top. It dances across the floor, its hum growing as in scene 1. Faint light comes up on Apu Mallku Tusuna. The condor cranes its neck. In her house, Inocencia straightens up and seems to be listening. As the top slows and tips over, light fades on the mountain. Inocencia turns her attention back to the dispachu.

MARCELINA: *(handing Suzicha a spindle)* Here, Suzicháy, you should be learning to spin.

SUZICHA: *(taking the spindle)* Yes, Grandma . . . Grandma, do you think he's gotten there yet?

MARCELINA: Oh yes, it's not that far and there's plenty of moonlight. They're probably making the dispachu right now.

(On the other level, Vicente enters, carrying a bottle of tragu and bundle of coca. Inocencia rises. Vicente hands her the tragu and coca, and she places them on the cloth. They both

remove their hats, embrace formally, and seat themselves on the floor, hats next to them.)

SUZICHA: Oh I hope they make it well, Grandma! I hope the Apu likes it.

MARCELINA: (*sighs thoughtfully, but keeps a cheerful face*) Oh, they will. Inocencia knows how. So does your grandfather, but right now he needs Inocencia to steady him. His heart is too full. (*sighs*) Mine too. And anyway, Inocencia knows these things better than either of us.

(As they speak Inocencia can be seen on the other level making the libation of tragu, including the four corners and center of the paper, as in the previous scene. Then she prepares four two-leafed coca k'intus, which she holds between the fingers of her left hand. She combines the four k'intus into two, then into one and blows over it. Light comes up on Apu Mallku Tusuna. The condor lifts its head. Then Inocencia places the k'intu in the center of the paper, and drives a pin through its center.)

SUZICHA: Why does Comadre Inocencia know more about these things, Grandma?

MARCELINA: Well, we all know how to blow our coca, and how to make an offering bundle for our own household. But people like Inocencia have a special gift for it. If they work at it—the way she has—they become healers . . . healers, or sorcerers.

SUZICHA: Sorcerers? Witches?

MARCELINA: Well, it's all the same medicine. Sorcery just turns it backwards. But of course, we trust our comadre . . .

SUZICHA: Why does she have the gift, Grandma?

MARCELINA: Who knows? That's just the way she is. When she was born they noticed that her feet were different. . . . You don't notice it now, under all the calluses (*she sighs and looks at her own callused feet*), but when she was young you could still see it. They say her mother was frightened by a lightning bolt when Inocencia was in her womb.

SUZICHA: Achakáu!

MARCELINA: So they weren't surprised when the baby was marked like that. Then later she turned out to be left-handed. When she was about your age, they say, she started to have dreams—powerful dreams. She couldn't get rid of them, so she had to learn to use them. And, that's how it started.

SUZICHA: Do you think they've finished making the dispachu yet, Grandma?

MARCELINA: Oh not yet, sweetheart! You can't hurry something like this. It's hard work, you have to keep your thoughts very strong and clear and choose the medicine very carefully. It's like cooking your soup, only it's a meal for the Earth and Mountain Lords. You know how, if you put the wrong things together in one soup, it tastes bad? Well, that's how it is with the dispachu. If you choose the wrong medicine your offering tastes bad—and the Mountain Lords spit it out and leave it on the ground!

SUZICHA: And if they like it, then they'll call my mother back here?

MARCELINA: Yes, because the medicine tells them what we want from them, and if they're pleased with it they'll help us in hopes of getting more.

(On the other level, Inocencia and Vicente are making the dispachu. Inocencia points to ingredients spread out on the cloth and Vicente takes them in his right hand, blows over them and places them on the paper, on top of the k'intu. Sometimes Inocencia hesitates, at other times Vicente pauses to rest, and they each have a shot of tragu. When the dispachu is completed Inocencia carefully folds up the ingredients in the paper, after pulling out the central pin. She marks the "head" with a small smudge of charcoal, blows over it intently, and hands it to Vicente. Light comes up a little stronger on Apu Mallku Tusuna. The condor cranes its neck hungrily. Vicente gives Inocencia a formal embrace and replaces his hat. She scrapes some glowing coals onto

a large potsherd and hands it to him. Vicente then leaves her
house, disappearing behind the platform. She sits down by
her fire and replaces her hat as the lights fade on her plat-
form.)

MARCELINA: Well, once they've finished making it, then comes
the hardest part.

SUZICHA: Hardest part?

MARCELINA: Your grandfather has to burn the offering. That's
how it passes to Mother Earth and the Mountain
Lords. Nothing—<u>nothing</u>—can go wrong now to
block that passage. He mustn't fumble when he
lights it, or place it wrong, so the coca isn't pointing
to the east. He has to make sure it starts burning—
but he mustn't look at it too long or the sight might
paralyze him.

SUZICHA: Achakáu! Grandma, I'm scared!

MARCELINA: Oh, he knows how to do it, little one. He won't stay
too long, and he won't look back. And we can help
by staying very quiet and chewing our coca leaves.
Maybe you can help me, little woman, little cook?

SUZICHA: Me? Yes, thank you, I'll try, Grandmother, urpicháy.

MARCELINA: *(handing her a k'intu)* Then hallpakusunchis,
Mamitáy.

SUZICHA: Yusulpayki. *(blows over the k'intu)* Pacha Mama,
Chiripata, and—Apu Mallku Tusuna. Eat well
tonight.

MARCELINA: Allinmi! That's good. You'll grow into it.

(Light comes up in the pasture as Vicente reappears. Very
intently and quickly he places the coals in a crevice of the
boulder. Then, checking the location of the offering's "head,"
he places the dispachu in the coals, moving his lips in an
invocation. Then he quickly turns away, again disappearing
behind a hillside/platform.)

SUZICHA: Grandma, you still haven't finished that story. What
happened to the girl? Did she ever go back to her parents?

MARCELINA: Come here, little sleepyhead. I'll tell you.

(Suzicha cuddles up next to Marcelina and puts her head in her lap. As Marcelina continues the story, the dispachu catches fire and burns. Lights come up on the Story Platform.)

MARCELINA: And so that girl lived there in the condor's nest, cold, miserable, and almost starving. She gave birth to a baby with black wings and condor feet, who died as soon as it saw the light of day. This was too much for her. She decided to deceive her husband and his family—and run away. She thought of a trick. "I'm going to wash the clothes in the stream," she told him, and then she left the condor village carrying their dirty clothes.

(The young woman runs across the Story Platform, carrying a bundle of clothes. There is light on her; the rest of the stage in shadow. She is very hurried and frightened. Suddenly she runs into a big green frog, K'ayra María.)

FROG: Well, allillanchu human girl, Mamitáy? And where might you be going? My stream's right here. Aren't you going to wash the clothes?

YOUNG WOMAN: Oh K'ayra María, I'm running away. I can't live in the condor village. I want to go home. I want to see my mother! I didn't know it would be like this.

FROG: Achakaláu! Poor little thing! Of course you want to leave! But you know it's not so easy to leave a condor. He'll find you, wherever you go.

YOUNG WOMAN: But I can't stay! I'll die if I stay!

FROG: Achakaláu, little girl, human girl. I'll try to help you. Give me your laundry. Maybe the sound of the washing will fool that husband of yours. At least you'll have a head start. Now go!

YOUNG WOMAN: K'ayra María, how can I thank you?

FROG: Just go! Run! Apuriy!

(The young woman runs off. The frog crouches in the shadow and begins noisily to wash the clothes. The mestizo/condor man runs in, the same light on him. He does not see the frog.)

CONDOR MAN: Mamáy! Little wife! Pretty human wife! Where are you?

FROG: *(from the shadow)* I'm here washing the clothes, sweetheart.

CONDOR MAN: Oh, well then, that's fine.

(He leaves. The frog continues to wash the clothes. The condor man reenters.)

CONDOR MAN: Urpicháy! Little runa wife! Have you finished washing the clothes?

FROG: Not yet, darling. They're plenty dirty!

(The condor man leaves, again reenters in a few moments.)

CONDOR MAN: Aren't you finished yet, little wife?

FROG: Not yet, my love. *(she slips away)*

(A brilliant hummingbird whirs onto the Story Platform with a more intense light following him as he flies in circles around the condor man.)

HUMMINGBIRD: *(rapidly)* Kharr! Bhirrr! Whirrrrr! Whirrrr!
Wherrrr? Wherrrr? WHERRRR'S your wife?
Wherrrr? Wherrrr? WHERRRR'S your wife?
She's rrrun rrrun RRRUN away!
Rrrun rrrun RRRRRRUN away!
RRRun home to motherrr! Kharrrr!
RRRun home to fatherrr! Whirrrr!
Kharrrr! Bhirrrr! Whirrrrr! Whirrrr!
Wherrrr? Wherrrr? WHERRRR'S your wife?
Wherrrr? Wherrrr? WheRRRR? WHERRRRRR?

(The condor man is furious. He tries to catch the hummingbird, who whirs around him some more and starts to fly away. The condor man gives up the chase and rushes to look for his wife in the shadow, but finds only dirty laundry.)

HUMMINGBIRD: Kharr! Whirr! She's gonnnne!

(Enraged and desperate, the condor man flies after the hummingbird.)

SUZICHA: *(excited and a little frightened)* Chaymantarí? And then what happens next, Grandma? Does she get home?

(Lights fade on the Story Platform as Vicente comes in the door. He is tired but exhilarated. He thinks they're talking about Adriana.)

VICENTE: She'll get home! Apu Mallku Tusuna has eaten! It's going to be all right.

(Lights fade.)

SCENE 10

Three months later (around December). The same path as in scene 4. It has been raining, and the ground is very muddy. Light is fading as the setting sun breaks through a cloudy sky. Vicente is on his way home. He has been weeding after dinner, and carries a small bundle with only a short hoe sticking out of it. Cipriano overtakes him, muddy and carrying a very large bundle.

CIPRIANO: *(calling as he catches up with Vicente)* Taytáy! Hamusayki, Vicente Taytáy! Suyamuway! Wait up!

VICENTE: *(stopping and turning)* Taytáy Cipriano, allillanchu? *(They both swing their bundles onto dryish spots on the ground.)* So you're back from Cuzco. I wondered whether the trucks would make it through today. They say the new road has washed out already. And it's been only three months since they finished it.

CIPRIANO: We almost <u>didn't</u> make it. All the roads are nothing but mud. Twice I thought we were going to slide right off a cliff. Everybody was screaming.

VICENTE: Atakáu!

CIPRIANO: And I had to walk all the way from T'ikaloma. The

trucks couldn't make it to Chiripata.

VICENTE: And with that big load . . . (*He eyes Cipriano's load curiously, but Cipriano ignores his interest.*) Well, maybe next year they'll have our road in better shape.

CIPRIANO: What an awful trip! We were packed in there like ducks in a crate. (*laughs ruefully*) A big market lady was sitting on my foot and she couldn't move either— for six hours we were like that, karahu! I could hardly walk when I got off! I thought my foot had disappeared, gone away somewhere, died maybe, but when I looked—there it was. Ay! (*shakes his foot*) And how it hurt when the feeling came back!

VICENTE: I've had that happen. It feels like a damned soul coming back to life.

CIPRIANO: Kukuchi! Atakáu! Anyway Taytáy, it's over with. I'll be glad to get home. Here's some bread for your little Suzicha. She can eat it with her dinner. (*Opens his bundle and pulls out a round piece of bread. Vicente peers into the bundle with reserved curiosity.*)

VICENTE: (*preparing to pick up his own bundle*) Yusulpayki, Taytáy Cipriano. We've already eaten dinner—I've just been doing a bit of weeding before the sun set. But Suzicha will be delighted. Now go on, go on! You must be tired!

CIPRIANO: (*deliberately*) You should be going too, Vicente Taytáy. You'll want to be home when your daughter arrives.

VICENTE: (*staring at Cipriano*) What?

CIPRIANO: Adriana was on the truck behind mine. It probably left about half an hour later.

VICENTE: In Cuzco? Are you sure it was Adriana?

CIPRIANO: (*amused*) Taytáy, of course I'm sure. She tried to get on our truck, but there was no room—everybody yelled at her to get on the other truck. She really didn't want to wait—seemed terrified. She even begged the truck driver to take her up in the cab—

but of course he wouldn't. So she got on the next truck and crouched way down inside with her shawl over her head.

VICENTE: (*who is standing dumbfounded*) Adriana . . .

CIPRIANO: So you'd better be going, Taytáy. (*He shoulders his bundle and starts off.*) Allinllaña!

VICENTE: Taytáy . . .

(*He shoulders his bundle in a daze and starts off. We see him wending his way home, as in scene 4. He is very agitated, and trots as fast as the muddy ground will allow.*)

SCENE 11

The house. Marcelina and Suzicha are tidying up after dinner. Suzicha is putting potato peels into the chipped pot for the dogs. Marcelina lifts the large ceramic pot off the fire onto the floor and covers its mouth with a small bowl. They are busy, not talking; neither seems very happy.

Vicente bursts through the door, very excited.

VICENTE: Mamáy! Suzicha!

MARCELINA: Hesus María! What's happening?

VICENTE: Mamáy! (*pauses to catch his breath*) She's coming. Adriana's coming. Cipriano saw her on a truck. She's coming from Cuzco.

SUZICHA: (*jumping to her feet*) Mamitáy!

MARCELINA: (*staring*) Achacháu. . . . Vicente, was he sure?

VICENTE: She tried to get on his truck, but it was full. He said she was in a hurry to get away!

SUZICHA: How soon will she be here? How soon?

(*Marcelina is dazedly getting to her feet.*)

VICENTE: He thought her truck must have been coming about half an hour behind his. Of course he didn't really know. And the trucks can only get as far as

T'ikaloma, so she'll have to walk from there.

MARCELINA: (*suddenly bursting into excitement*) Then she'll be tired and hungry! (*She picks up the soup pot and puts it back on the fire.*) Vicente! Can you peel some more ch'uñu? Susana! Blow on the fire, can't you? We'll have to heat up the leftover soup.

SUZICHA: (*rushing to the q'uncha*) Where's the blowing tube?

(*Vicente is stepping across to the q'uncha as Suzicha runs around looking for the blowing tube. They collide, spilling a basket of potatoes, which roll across the floor. All three laugh a bit hysterically. Vicente and Marcelina frantically pick up the potatoes; Suzicha grabs the opportunity to rush outside. In a moment she is back.*)

SUZICHA: She's coming! She's coming! I can see her coming over Muqumuqu!

(*Silence and calm descend as the adults put a lid on their excitement. Vicente sits down on the bench and begins to work on a rope, Marcelina finishes picking up the potatoes, then takes her place by the fire and stirs the soup. Suzicha tries to run out the door.*)

MARCELINA: Suzicha!

(*Suzicha reluctantly sits down to peel ch'uñu. Although all three are expectant, the two adults maintain expressionless faces. Adriana's voice calls at the door.*)

ADRIANA: Hamusayki Mamáy! Hamusayki, Taytáy!

MARCELINA: Pasayukuy!

(*Adriana enters, soaking wet, dressed in mestiza clothing. She is very bedraggled. She stands looking at her family. Her parents maintain their calm detached demeanor and glance casually at Adriana, maintaining for the most part an averted gaze; Suzicha crouches like some kind of joyous but suppressed little animal.*)

ADRIANA: Mother, good evening. Father, good evening. Allillanchu?

VICENTE: Allillanmi, Daughter. So you've come back?

ADRIANA: Yes, I've come back.

VICENTE: (*puts down the rope and looks at Adriana*) I'm glad.

*(He gets up and approaches her; she takes off her hat, they
embrace formally, touching each other only on the shoulders
but with great feeling. Vicente returns to his seat and Marcelina rises, takes off her hat and approaches Adriana for
the same greeting. Adriana begins to cry softly as they
embrace, again formally. As Marcelina withdraws, Suzicha
leaps forward and hugs her mother, almost knocking her
down.)*

SUZICHA: Mamáy! Mamitáy! You're back! You're back!

ADRIANA: Wawáy! How I missed you! Ay Suzicháy!

*(Marcelina is rummaging among the clothes on a beam
above the bed, and pulls down a skirt, shawl, and sweater
for Adriana.)*

MARCELINA: (*with loving authority*) You must be freezing.
(*feels her hand*) Alaláu! What a mess! Here, dry off—
and put on some real clothes.

VICENTE: —runa clothes. (*He is rummaging around for the
tragu. He finds the bottle and glass, begins to pour
a shot.*)

MARCELINA: Vicente! Let her change her clothes first.

VICENTE: (*good-humoredly corking the bottle*) Riki, riki.

*(Adriana and Suzicha release each other. Adriana moves
into the shadow by the bed to change her clothes. Suzicha
runs over to the fire and checks the soup.)*

MARCELINA: Is it ready yet?

SUZICHA: Almost.

*(She wipes out the enamel bowl. Marcelina empties a pot of
boiled potatoes onto a woven cloth. Vicente puts a small*

bowl of salt next to it. Adriana has changed her clothes, and emerges from the shadow looking more like her old self.)

MARCELINA: Sit down child, and eat some dinner. *(She puts a folded shawl on the floor.)*

ADRIANA: Thank you, Mother. *(sinks wearily down on the shawl)* Hananów . . . I'm so tired. *(peels and eats a boiled potato)*

(Marcelina tests the soup and removes the pot from the fire. She ladles soup into the enamel bowl and gives it to Adriana with the spoon.)

ADRIANA: Añañau! Oh Mother, how good it smells!

(Vicente closes the door and lights the candle; they do the evening greeting as in scene 2.)

MARCELINA: *(removing her hat, motioning with her right hand toward Vicente and then Suzicha)* Buenas noches, Taytáy. Buenas noches, Hawacháy. Buenas noches, Adriana.

VICENTE / SUZICHA / ADRIANA: *(simultaneously)* Buenas noches, Mamáy. Buenas noches, Hawacháy. Buenas noches, Adriana. / Buenas noches, Machuláy. Buenas noches, Auláy. Buenas noches, Mamáy. / Buenas noches, Mamáy. Buenas noches, Taytáy. Buenas noches, Suzicháy.

ADRIANA: I missed this food!

VICENTE: Indian food.

MARCELINA: I'll bet they don't have potatoes like this in town— *(picks up a potato, then another)* puma maki . . . puka mama . . .

ADRIANA: Yes, I did miss them.

VICENTE: Tell us, my daughter, how were the roads? Did you have a good trip?

ADRIANA: Awful. It rained all the way. They put a tarpaulin over us to keep the rain off, but then I could hardly breathe. And we could all feel the truck slipping and sliding in the mud. I was so glad to get off . . . I've had enough of trucks. They scare me and the smell makes me dizzy.

SUZICHA: I like the smell!

ADRIANA: Not for hours on end! You don't know how it is. And in town the air smells of it all the time. Especially Cuzco. In Cuzco it was the worst.

(Adriana has finished eating. Suzicha takes her bowl and places it near the q'uncha. Marcelina wraps up the cloth of boiled potatoes. She then sits next to Adriana and Suzicha, and opens her coca bundle. Vicente opens his coca bag. Adriana is empty-handed. Marcelina gives her two large handfuls of coca, which she holds in her lap. Then, holding the coca in the folds of her skirt, Adriana rises to put a pinch of coca in the q'uncha.)

ADRIANA: *(quietly, as she sits down)* Wasi Mama. I'm back.

(They settle comfortably; while they talk, they chew coca and exchange k'intus.)

VICENTE: Well Adriana, so now you've seen Cuzco.

MARCELINA: *(chuckling)* I remember how you used to beg your father to take you, when you were Suzicha's age. One morning you followed him halfway to the truck stop.

VICENTE: Howling like a kukuchi. Yes, I used to go to Cuzco back then, every once in awhile. No more.

MARCELINA: I only went once, a long time ago.

VICENTE: She was terrified.

MARCELINA: So many people! All strangers. And traffic. And the houses high as hills! I didn't know which way to turn. Everything seemed like a blur.

VICENTE: I had to lead her by the hand.

ADRIANA: Yes, I felt like that at first. It got better but I never did feel all right there. Yet . . . you can get everything in the big market! And I saw the Cathedral and so many Inca walls . . .

MARCELINA: We heard rumors that you were in Sicuani—and now you come from Cuzco?

ADRIANA: Well . . . when we—José Luis and I—when we left here we went to Sicuani because he's from there. And his sister has a store there. But it didn't work out for us. After awhile we gave up and went to Cuzco.

VICENTE: What didn't work out?

ADRIANA: We thought we could make a home there, living from his salary. He had a little rented room near his sister's house, so we started living there. We thought that after awhile we could buy enough land to build a house on. We were so excited! We thought that after awhile we'd come for Suzicha—and (*to her parents*) maybe you too if you wanted—and take you back to live in town. In a concrete house with windows and a wooden floor and a television.

SUZICHA: Achacháu!

ADRIANA: And José Luis would have his own pickup truck . . . and we'd come driving back to visit Chiripata on the road he helped build. . . . We were so excited and happy, it was like being drunk.

(*Vicente appears about to make a sarcastic response, but he restrains himself.*)

ADRIANA: Oh Father, of course it didn't work out that way. But it was wonderful being together. (*sighs*) It was never really bad with José Luis. That wasn't the problem. Ay sunqulláy!

MARCELINA: Then what was the problem, Wawacháy?

ADRIANA: I couldn't get used to living in town. I felt sad all the time, a big heaviness in my heart. And town didn't like me. Not the people. Not the things. I was afraid to go anywhere. I was always afraid a car would come up behind me. And I thought the smell—oh the gasoline and, and the shit!—would suffocate me. It felt as though the walls on either side of the street were going to close in and eat me.

MARCELINA: Achakaláu!

ADRIANA: Well, that part did get better, but the heavy feeling never left my heart . . . I guess that was what killed the baby—that and I guess all the bad smells . . .

VICENTE: (*abruptly*) Baby?

ADRIANA: (*steeling herself*) We didn't realize it when we left, but I was already expecting a baby. We were so happy.

VICENTE: (*flabbergasted*) How?

MARCELINA: How! Old Man, how does anybody?

VICENTE: I mean—

MARCELINA: (*calm but forceful, leaning toward him*) Quiet now. Upa. Let her tell us.

ADRIANA: There's not much to tell. We were happy about it. We lived in his room and cooked on a primus burner. There was a water faucet in the courtyard. He was working on a job near to town, so he came home every night. But I felt lonely and frightened during the day—usually I went to his sister's but that wasn't much better . . .

VICENTE: (*impatiently*) So what happened?

ADRIANA: I'm telling you. One day after the rains had started I was crossing the street and I thought I heard a car behind me. I was so frightened that I ran to the sidewalk, right into a big duck!

(*Suzicha giggles.*)

ADRIANA: Yes, everybody laughed. I went flying right into a mud puddle. The duck was hurt, and its owner—he was this skinny little misti with a wispy mustache—came over and started yelling at me while I was still lying there. Then a big fat market lady in a red skirt came over and started yelling at <u>him</u>. He backed off, and she—the market lady, they call her Puka Juana—helped me get up and walked me home. It seemed like the whole world was standing there laughing.

SUZICHA: (*jumping to her feet*) How awful!

ADRIANA: That's when the pains started. Puka Juana was very kind, stayed with me as long as she could. We sent for José Luis's sister, but she was too busy and never came.

MARCELINA: Atakáu!

ADRIANA: And so that's how it was. The baby came too soon. Much, much too soon. By the time José Luis got home it was over. Hinayá!

VICENTE: (*deeply shocked*) Manan allinchu! Daughter, what a bad business. That's a bad place!

ADRIANA: It got worse. José Luis was so upset. He cried all night. The next morning—it's unbelievable—he really never drinks—but . . . he got drunk on his way to work and couldn't even handle the bulldozer. He drove it right into a swamp.

VICENTE: Karahu!

ADRIANA: So that was the end of his job. The foreman had some of the other men carry him home and told him never to come back. He couldn't even walk. The next day he couldn't remember what he did.

VICENTE: Damned misti! I told you—

ADRIANA: Father! He's not really like that! The grief made him crazy! I never saw him drunk before or after!

SUZICHA: What happened to the bulldozer, Mama?

ADRIANA: I don't know. We heard that it took them two days to get it out of the mud.

MARCELINA: The swamp must have wanted to keep it.

SUZICHA: That nice snorty bulldozer. What a shame!

ADRIANA: Yes, José Luis felt very ashamed. Then in a couple of weeks the landlord turned us out on the street. We had no money left—José Luis even had to sell his nice shoes—and everybody was talking about how he got drunk and wrecked the bulldozer.

VICENTE: Hesus María!

MARCELINA: Is that when you went to Cuzco?

ADRIANA: Not quite. We moved in with his sister, slept in a little corner of her kitchen. I cooked for her and José Luis helped in the store. (*lapses into silence*)

MARCELINA: Ay taytalláy!

ADRIANA: In a way, that was the worst part. His sister hated me and was disgusted with him. She was ashamed to have me for a sister-in-law. When strangers came into the store she tried to pretend I was just a servant girl from the countryside.

MARCELINA: Karahu!

ADRIANA: She used to speak Spanish just to humiliate me, because I couldn't understand. I tried to learn, but somehow my mind just couldn't hold onto it. I felt so ignorant, and I got so clumsy. I don't know, I'm not usually clumsy—but there, in town, I was. I never could light her kerosene stove. Once I almost set my hair on fire! Oh, and I missed you so much, especially Suzicha! (*to Suzicha*) And there was no way to bring you unless you hired out as a kitchen girl and . . . when I saw what that was like . . .

SUZICHA: Well, I do know how to cook now—

VICENTE: It's not a life for us! Now you know why.

ADRIANA: Yes, I couldn't get used to it.

MARCELINA: Achakaláu!

ADRIANA: José Luis was so tense all the time, always in a bad mood. He was mad at his sister for treating me badly—and, and I'm sure he was embarrassed by me, because I couldn't do anything. I don't know, I felt in a daze all the time. Nothing was clear. And I felt so heavy. I would pick something up and it would slip out of my hands.

MARCELINA: That's just not like you.

VICENTE: (*to Marcelina*) She must have been sick.

ADRIANA: Two weeks ago we gave up, decided to start over again in Cuzco. José Luis has a cousin who sells fish in the market, so we went to him. He's a nice man. He and his family live right in their market stall, but they made room for us. We had to sleep curled up on top of each other, like a lot of puppies.

SUZICHA: (*laughing*) Like this? (*snuggles up to her mother*)

ADRIANA: (*smiling at Suzicha*) For a few days I felt better. We walked all over Cuzco and saw all the churches, and the Plaza de Armas—everything!

SUZICHA: Añañau!

ADRIANA: Then José Luis started to make money. For a few days he worked as a street porter. He was happy to be earning again, even though it meant carrying loads for Cuzco mistis, like an animal. Nobody knew that he used to be almost a professional, driving a bulldozer.

VICENTE: (*sarcastic, under his breath to Marcelina*) Pobrecito!

ADRIANA: A few days ago he got a job making adobes at a construction site. He felt hopeful again but I—the bad feeling, that heaviness, came back to me. I tried to help sell fish, but somehow my mind got all cloudy again, and my hands wouldn't hold onto anything. I knew I couldn't stay there.

MARCELINA: That's when you came back?

ADRIANA: I stayed on for a few days. I tried to talk to José Luis but he couldn't hear me. He got angry, said everything he'd suffered had been for my sake. So I knew I would have to leave.

VICENTE: Chiripata called you back.

ADRIANA: Yes, I had to get back here. This morning—imagine, it was only this morning!—I said that I would wash José Luis's other shirt—he has two shirts—and . . . well, I just ran away. I was so afraid he would guess and follow me to the truck stop. But he didn't. I was on the last truck, so if he did guess, he was too late to follow me today . . . and then ay, what a trip! But now I'm here. It's over. (*she sags, exhausted*) Hinayá. . .

SUZICHA: (*leaning against her comfortingly*) Mamitáy . . .

(Sounds of a downpour and thunder. They all look at each other, startled.)

VICENTE: Wau! What a downpour! This will wash out half the roads! And you know, José Luis won't be able to get through. Not for a week at least!

MARCELINA: You can rest easy, Waway.

VICENTE: Our Apu Mallku Tusuna is keeping him away.

(Marcelina gets up and clears a space on the bed.)

MARCELINA: Come to bed, dear. You're exhausted.

(Adriana climbs onto the bed like a sleepwalker and collapses. Suzicha takes off her mother's sandals and covers her with a blanket. She is sound asleep.)

VICENTE: Good, good, she needs to sleep.

MARCELINA: I guess we should sleep too, Taytalláy. Especially you, Suzicháy.

SUZICHA: Grandma! I can't possibly sleep. I'm too happy! I feel like running and dancing!

VICENTE: *(laughing)* Me too! I'm too excited to sleep.

MARCELINA: Well, to tell the truth, I'm not sleepy either.

VICENTE: *(jumps up happily and pats Marcelina on the hip)* Let's dance! Let's make Carnival! Let's wake up the ayllu and tell them Adriana's home!

MARCELINA: *(loud whisper)* Achacháu! *(lovingly swats him)* You crazy old dog! We'll wake her up. Come, let's just sit down by the fire.

(Vicente picks up the tragu bottle and sits by the fire. Suzicha runs over to peer at her mother and then sits down near Marcelina. Vicente pours himself a shot.)

VICENTE: Salud! Tomanki!

MARCELINA: *(indulgently)* Yes, yes, tomakuy.

(More sounds of rain and thunder.)

SUZICHA: So you think the trucks won't be able to get through for awhile?

VICENTE: How could they! Nothing'll move for two weeks, maybe a month.

MARCELINA: You hope . . .

VICENTE: Siguru! They could hardly get through today. By the time they are moving again that misti will probably have forgotten Adriana . . .

MARCELINA: Taytáy, he'll come. Now or later. Remember what Inocencia told us. And everything else she said was true—the loss . . . she saw it clearly. Why should she be wrong now?

VICENTE: Well, mmmm—then he'll come later. There's no way he can get through in the next week or so. We have some time, anyway, before he gets here.

MARCELINA: When he comes he'll try to carry her off again.

VICENTE: I'll take care of that—if he does come, if he makes it through the mud.

(He takes another drink; offers a shot to Marcelina, who brushes it aside. He drinks her shot as well. The bottle is empty.)

VICENTE: *(shaking the bottle upside down)* Karahu!

SUZICHA: Grandmother, what happened in the story when the condor followed the girl home?

MARCELINA: I never did finish telling you, did I? About the runa's daughter and the condor qatay.

SUZICHA: That's right.

VICENTE: Condor qatay kasqa? Is that the story you're telling? Ha! They sure got him at the end! Karahu! Served him right! *(scornfully)* A condor son-in-law! Ha!

MARCELINA: Upa, Old Man. Let me tell it.

SUZICHA: That's right, you tell it, Grandma.

MARCELINA: Well, the condor followed the hummingbird, flying on his big black wings. But the girl had a head start. She ran home as fast as she could, right into her parents' house.

SUZICHA: What did her parents say, Grandma?

VICENTE: They had a party! Karahu!

MARCELINA: Vicente, upa! They were glad, but the humming-bird told them they had to make a plan. The condor was sure to follow.

SUZICHA: Achacháu!

MARCELINA: The condor landed on the ground some distance from their house, and transformed himself back into a beautiful young man. He wanted to impress his father-in-law.

(Light comes up on the Story Platform. The light and action are partial, as though the action is shared between the family and the story time. On the Story Platform sits a big steaming cauldron. The young woman runs onto the platform and into the house. Her parents embrace her joyously. Then the hummingbird whirrs onto the platform, circles them, and flies off. The young woman and her mother begin stoking the fire under the cauldron. The hummingbird leads the mestizo/condor man in as a mestizo and flies off. The mestizo/condor stands at the threshold; pantomimes knocking on a door.)

MARCELINA: And so that condor son-in-law came to the door, and knocked.

(Vicente raps on a large cooking pot.)

CONDOR MAN: Hamusayki! Little wife, pretty runa wife, are you there?

YOUNG WOMAN: Just a minute dear, I'm getting dressed.

(She and her mother put more sticks on the fire, blow and fan it. Her father gets a poncho.)

MARCELINA: So the condor waited for awhile. But you know what they were really doing inside? They were boiling water in a big, big cauldron!

VICENTE: Ha ha! What a trick!

MARCELINA: Then after awhile the condor knocked again.

(Condor man pantomimes knocking. Vicente raps on the pot again.)

CONDOR MAN: Ñachu? Ñachu?

VICENTE: Ready yet? Aren't you ready yet?

YOUNG WOMAN: Manaraq! Manaraq, urpicháy!

MARCELINA: Not yet! Not yet, sweetheart! And so, the condor waited awhile longer. And inside the house they kept stoking the fire.

(The young woman and her mother work furiously at the fire. The father stands impatiently with the poncho.)

MARCELINA: Then after awhile the condor knocked again.

(Condor man pantomimes knocking. Vicente raps on the pot again.)

CONDOR MAN: Ñachu? Ñachu?

VICENTE: Ready yet? Aren't you ready yet?

YOUNG WOMAN: Manaraq! Manaraq, urpicháy!

MARCELINA: Not yet! Not yet, sweetheart! And so, the condor waited—but not too long. He was getting impatient.

(The young woman's father spreads the poncho over the cauldron. The girl and her mother draw back expectantly and sit near the cauldron. Her father stands waiting.)

MARCELINA: And so the condor knocked again.

(Condor man pantomimes knocking. Vicente raps on the pot again.)

CONDOR MAN: Ñachu? Ñachu?

VICENTE: Ready yet? Aren't you ready yet?

YOUNG WOMAN: Listullaña, urpicháy! Pasayukuy!

MARCELINA: I'm all ready! Come right in, sweetheart! And so they received him very nicely.

THE FATHER: Pasakuy! Hamuway, Qatayniy! PasaYUkuy! *(embraces him formally)* Yusulpayki VIsitamu-WAnki, QaTAYniy! MaNAchu saMUwaq? TiyaYUkuy Wiraqucha! *(indicates that he should sit on the poncho-covered cauldron)*

(Vicente has jumped to his feet and pantomimes receiving and embracing a guest.)

VICENTE: Like this—Come IN, my DEAR, my SON-in-law. Come IN, THANK you dear SON-in-law, you're VIsiting me! Aren't you TIRED? Won't you PLEASE have a SEAT?

MARCELINA: And so they asked him to sit down.

VICENTE: TiyaYUkuy, QaTAYniy!

(The condor man sits on the cauldron, not seeing the steam that is beginning to rise from it. For a moment he is suspended on the edge, and the three in the Story House pause in suspense. Marcelina, Suzicha, and Vicente pause in suspense as well, staring at the spot where Vicente had pantomimed the cauldron.)

(Then, with a great screech, the condor man falls into the cauldron with a great boiling, hissing sound and a burst of steam.)

VICENTE: Ha ha ha! Phultín! *(capers about the imagined cauldron)* Ha ha ha! In he went! Wau! Bhouuph! Pshh-hhh!

(On the Story Platform the mestizo turns back into a condor as he writhes in the steaming cauldron. The family shouts "Hiyalli! Hiyalli!" and dances around him, forcing him back under the boiling water as he tries to struggle.)

MARCELINA: And then they knew! They knew—

SUZICHA: Knew what?

VICENTE: That it was a condor all the time! Ha!

(A naked torso bobs out of the cauldron and falls back in again. Light fades on the Story Platform.)

MARCELINA: *(looking back, at Suzicha)* That condor boiled until all his feathers fell off, and there he was, naked, like any boiled chicken!

SUZICHA: *(distressed)* And then what happened to him?

(Vicente laughs and capers. He pantomimes grasping a hunk of meat and devouring it, using the same gesture used in the condor dance in scene 6.)

MARCELINA: *(calmly)* He was eaten. He was devoured by his wife's parents.

(The story family finishes its celebration by reaching into the pot and devouring the naked condor. Suzicha gazes wide-eyed at Vicente, who laughs back at her.)

MARCELINA: And that's the way it was, little granddaughter. That's all I know.

(The two adults settle down again by the fire, shaking their heads in amusement. Suzicha begins to run to her sleeping mother, then turns abruptly to look at her grandparents.)

(Lights fade.)

SCENE 12

Two days have passed. Suzicha and Marcelina are in the pasture, late in the afternoon. They are trying to keep the rain off as they keep an eye on the animals. Both of them are far more relaxed, especially Suzicha, who has regained her old liveliness.

MARCELINA: Alaláu! This rain'll chill me to the bone!

SUZICHA: And the ground so slippery and slidy! The pig nearly went sliding right into the ravine!

MARCELINA: Llu-uushkallaña! Better keep an eye on the sheep. A sheep can just stand there and drown. The pig's not so stupid.

SUZICHA: *(looking off in the direction of the road)* So much for the new road, Grandma! It's nothing but mud.

MARCELINA: They say all the roads are washed out. Nobody's going anywhere. It may be weeks before any trucks are moving again.

(Cipriano darts up, carrying a hoe. He is excited.)

CIPRIANO: Marcelina Mamáy! Allillanchu?

MARCELINA: Allillanmi, Cipriano Taytáy. And where are you going in such a hurry?

CIPRIANO: Where does it look like? I'm here aren't I?

MARCELINA: *(remembering the incident with the sheep)* What now, Taytáy?

CIPRIANO: Mamáy, I just saw something interesting—something you might like to know.

MARCELINA: *(perplexed)* —that I might like to know?

CIPRIANO: I was just coming down from my fields on Lukiluma and I saw—

MARCELINA: Not our sheep, Taytáy!

CIPRIANO: *(too excited to contain his news any longer)* Mamáy, I saw that misti—that José Luis Flores Quispe—coming over the old high path.

(Both Marcelina and Suzicha are amazed.)

SUZICHA: Mamáy!

MARCELINA: Hesus María! Are you sure?

CIPRIANO: Siguru! I came over here out of my way just to tell you. I have to hurry now, my wife's waiting for me! *(He starts to leave, pauses to call over his shoulder.)* And Mamáy, you should make him pay for the potato seeds and fertilizer! He owes it to you! And to Mama Inocencia as well!

MARCELINA: Allinllaña, Cipriano Taytáy. Thanks for telling us. *(hurriedly picks up her sling)* Achacháu! Suzicha, can he really be coming so soon! Quick, let's round up the sheep! And the alpacas! I'll get them! Apuriy!

SUZICHA: He must have walked all the way!

MARCELINA: So fast!

(Inocencia enters in the opposite direction from Cipriano, hurrying along as she did in scene 6.)

INOCENCIA: Aumarya, Comadre! Aumarya, Suzicháy! Comadre, he's here! He's here already! I was coming up from the riverside and I saw him—José Luis—coming over the old high path!

MARCELINA: Cipriano just told us! We're rounding up our animals! It's unbelievable! How could he get here so fast!

INOCENCIA: The coca said he'd follow Adriana. And here he is. I have to hurry. Allinllaña, Comadre! Allinllaña, Wawáy!

(She leaves, still moving in the opposite direction from Cipriano. Marcelina and Suzicha rush off, Marcelina whirling her sling, Suzicha calling the pigs.)

SUZICHA: Khuchi! Yau, khuchi!

(Lights fade.)

SCENE 13

The house. Vicente has placed a small wooden stool (like a foot stool) in front of the bench and has his coca cloth spread out upon it. He is wearing a fine poncho and ch'ullu, and a fancy scarf with fringes. He sits on the bench doing phukuy (blowing his coca) with great concentration. Adriana enters, carrying the water jug.

VICENTE: It seems your husband's already coming over the old high path. *(dryly)* He must have sprouted wings. *(as Adriana stops in amazement)* Well, come in! We have to prepare ourselves.

(Adriana gives a start; her reaction is both joyous and frightened. She puts down the water and rushes to the clothes rack (beam over the bed), where she pulls down a particularly fine skirt and shawl. She puts the skirt over the one she is wearing, and sits down on the edge of the bed in order to comb out, and rebraid, her hair.)

VICENTE: *(amused and firm)* Your hair is fine, little pigeon. Now build up the fire and put on the water. The tired man will want his soup.

(Adriana goes over to the stove, and, crouching before it, begins blowing on the coals through a tube, feeding in twigs as the fire catches. Vicente prepares a k'intu with great deliberation and blows over it in the direction of Apu Mallku Tusuna.)

VICENTE: Apu Mallku Tusuna,
          Fog Breather, Star Thrower,
          You've brought a thief to my door.
          Now help me catch him!

(He chews the k'intu. Adriana, who had paused as Vicente spoke of the "thief," resumes blowing. Suzicha bursts in the door.)

SUZICHA: Mother! He's coming! *(She rushes to her mother's side, both protectively and as if seeking protection.)*

ADRIANA: *(puts down the blowing tube, moves over next to the stove, drawing Suzicha to her)* Don't be afraid, my own little shepherdess. I won't leave you again.

(She begins to peel potatoes. Suzicha takes off her wet shawl and begins to blow on the fire, still huddled in her mother's skirts. Marcelina hurries in.)

MARCELINA: Buenas tardes, Taytáy. Buenas tardes, Adriana.

(She looks carefully at Vicente, and goes deliberately to the clothes rack, where she too pulls down a good skirt and shawl and very quickly puts them on. She sits on the floor and begins to peel potatoes, blocking access to Adriana from the door. Vicente folds up the coca cloth, and sits waiting.)

(José Luis's voice is heard calling.)

JOSÉ LUIS: Yau! Mamáy! Hamusayki!

SUZICHA: *(panicky, jumps up)* You can't come in! We're not ready!

(Marcelina grabs her and sits her down by the fire.)

VICENTE: *(muttering)* Karahu!

JOSÉ LUIS: *(a note of exhaustion in his voice)* Mamáy,

hamusaykiman!

MARCELINA: (*heartily*) Come in!

VICENTE: Pasayukuy!

(*José Luis comes in. He is wearing the same thin jacket and polyester pants, as well as a felt hat. He has rubber sandals on his feet. He is very bedraggled; wet, cold and muddy. Though exhausted, he is trying to make the best entrance he can. It is his intention to retrieve Adriana and take her back to the town; he has not thought through the situation farther than that. He looks urgently toward Adriana, who stops peeling potatoes and glances furtively once under her fringed hat. Thereafter she keeps her face averted.*)

VICENTE: (*rising*) So you've come to visit me again.

JOSÉ LUIS: Vicente Taytáy. (*to Marcelina*) Mamáy. (*cranes his neck to look at Adriana, who averts her eyes*) Mamitáy . . . ? (*Marcelina shifts position to obstruct his view of Adriana.*)

MARCELINA: Wiraqucha, buenas tardes.

VICENTE: (*with courteous formality*) So you've come, walking through the mud and rain, all that long way, to pay me a visit. Come in, come in my dear, don't just stand there little brother, Wayqíy. Surely you're tired.

JOSÉ LUIS: (*feeling at a loss, still trying to catch Adriana's eye*) Yes, Vicente Taytáy. Thank you. It was a long journey.

VICENTE: Then sit down and rest, little brother. Sit down and warm yourself.

MARCELINA: (*sitting solid as a boulder, hearty and forceful*) That's right, Wiraqucha, tiyayukuy! (*to Vicente*) Achakaláu, how wet he is, Vicente! Bring the small stool over here, so he can sit closer to the fire. (*to José Luis*) Wiraqucha! Don't you want to dry yourself by our fire?

(*Vicente places the low stool about three feet from the fire.*)

JOSÉ LUIS: (*reluctant to sit, remains standing awkwardly*)

Thank you, thank you very much. But I—I've come to talk to Adriana.

(Adriana does not look at him. Marcelina does not budge, and feigns a look of surprise. Vicente deliberately steps closer to him.)

VICENTE: Achacháu! Don't joke with us, little brother. Surely you learned better manners in Mayumarca! My little pigeon is snug in the nest here, safe in her father's house. *(to Adriana, with imperious benevolence)* Adriana, urpicháy! Hurry up with the soup!

(Adriana immediately returns to her potato peeling, without looking up. Suzicha follows suit, glancing defensively now and then at José Luis.)

JOSÉ LUIS: *(in dismay)* Well . . . then, I'll sit down. Forgive me, thank you, I'll sit down. *(he sits)*

VICENTE: *(sitting on the bench, opening his coca bag)* Allinmi, allinmi. That's right, sit and rest, little brother.

MARCELINA: Good, rest and warm yourself. Ay! The soup won't be ready for awhile—but we can fix you some hot tea. Suzicha, I picked some chamomile. You'll find it in the corner back there. *(to José Luis)* That'll warm you up.

(Suzicha retrieves the sprig of chamomile and an enamel mug.)

JOSÉ LUIS: *(trying to insist, fighting exhaustion)* Thank you.

MARCELINA: *(solicitous)* There now! A hot drink will do you good.

JOSÉ LUIS: Now, forgive me, Taytáy, Mamáy, but I have to sp—

(He pauses as Adriana, eyes still averted, takes the mug with chamomile from Suzicha and pours hot water in it. She hands the mug to Marcelina.)

ADRIANA: Mamáy! Here's the gentleman's tea.

MARCELINA: Thank you daughter, Ususíy! *(Reaching, she hands the mug to José Luis.)* Here you are! The mug is hot, you can warm those cold hands on it.

JOSÉ LUIS: (*Takes the mug and cups his hands around it. In spite of himself he finds the warmth welcome.*) Yusulpayki.

VICENTE: (*adds coca leaves to the wad in his mouth; does not offer any to José Luis*) You've had a long walk from Cuzco. How long did it take you?

JOSÉ LUIS: Two days. (*sips his tea*) I spent last night in Machubamba—my sister's compadre lives there. I slept by their fireplace and left this morning before it got light.

VICENTE: All the way from Machubamba in one day! And over the old high path in this weather!

MARCELINA: Achacháu! That's fast walking!

JOSÉ LUIS: I didn't have any trouble on the old high path, except for the mud. (*relaxing a little, sipping his tea*) I expected fog or rain coming over the last pass but the weather actually improved. I could see all of Chiripata spread out below me.

VICENTE: Ah, that's because our Apu Mallku Tusuna wanted you to come.

JOSÉ LUIS: Well, I'm grateful for that. I hope he'll be as helpful on our way back to Cuzco. (*trying again to look at Adriana*) Especially if we have to walk.

VICENTE: Amayá little brother! You've just arrived. Why talk about leaving?

JOSÉ LUIS: Taytáy, forgive me, but I've come for Adriana—

VICENTE: (*deliberately*) —come for Adriana. . . . Slowly, Wayqíy, slowly. We do these things slowly in Chiripata.

MARCELINA: (*as if saddened*) Ay taytalláy! Don't they have any manners in Mayumarca?

VICENTE: Don't blame him, Mamáy. Remember, he's an orphan boy. How could this little wakcha learn manners herding pigs in Sicuani? No wonder he has no idea how to come asking for a wife!

(José Luis is stung, puts the mug down on the floor.)

MARCELINA: *(taking the mug)* You're very welcome, dear boy! Hinallatapis.

(Suzicha suppresses a giggle. Adriana continues peeling potatoes, eyes averted.)

JOSÉ LUIS: Taytáy, I mean—

VICENTE: Little brother, I understand that it's confusing. Let me help you. Even though you came before like a thief—like a fox after chickens—or shall we say, pigeons—I'll forgive you. I understand that you're a strong, good-hearted orphan boy who didn't know any better.

JOSÉ LUIS: *(trying to interrupt)* Taytáy—

VICENTE: But our little pigeon got away from you and came flying home to us. Why should I let you steal her again?

MARCELINA: Why indeed?

SUZICHA: And she wouldn't go again, anyhow!

(Adriana finally reacts, grabbing Suzicha's wrist to quiet her.)

ADRIANA / MARCELINA: Sssst! Upa!

VICENTE: *(rising, still holding his coca bag)* Here in Chiripata you have to come asking for a wife like a real person. Not like a fox, but a real person. *(He begins to pace.)* You come with your parents—your taytamama— bringing presents—at the very least bringing coca and tragu—fine tender coca leaves and bottles of strong sweet tragu.

JOSÉ LUIS: I—

VICENTE: Ay, little brother, I understand. Your parents are gone. Achakaláu! Died and left you. But there must be someone—surely an uncle, a cousin, your elder sister—

JOSÉ LUIS: *(winces)* Taytáy, I know—

VICENTE: You mean—? Ah, little brother, I misunderstood. Are they waiting outside? Not out in the rain, karahu!

They should come in. We're ready for them—

(He goes to the door and peers out. José Luis looks desperately at Adriana.)

JOSÉ LUIS: *(whispering)* Adriana! *(She does not respond; he tries to start toward her.)*

VICENTE: *(interposing himself between José Luis and Adriana)* No, no. Nobody at all. Poor orphan boy.

MARCELINA: Achakaláu.

JOSÉ LUIS: *(annoyed and embarrassed)* Taytáy! I—

VICENTE: *(walking toward the bench)* Then surely you came alone. Poor wakcha! You decided to bring the gifts yourself. Ay, little brother, you didn't need to leave them outside!

MARCELINA: *(rising)* Out in the rain! *(She goes to the door and peers out.)* No, nothing.

VICENTE: *(to Marcelina)* Ay! What a problem! No family! No gifts! How can this poor orphan boy ever ask for a wife!

MARCELINA: What can he do? Whatever can he do? Poor little wakcha! Ay sunqulláy!

(She walks over toward the bed as Vicente approaches the q'uncha, as if circling around José Luis.)

VICENTE: You know, if you were really asking for a wife, I would have to question you. That's how we do it here. It's our custom. I'd have to be hard on you. So you'd understand your obligation to us.

JOSÉ LUIS: *(defensively)* Taytáy, what do I have to hide? I'm not afraid of questions.

VICENTE: Well sir, how old are you?

JOSÉ LUIS: I'm twenty-five. I have my identification papers. I finished my military service—as you know, Taytáy. I'm healthy, and I work hard.

VICENTE: *(amused)* Not so fast! You work hard, and you steal pigeons. Do you steal anything else? Have you ever been in jail?

JOSÉ LUIS: Jail? Of course not!

VICENTE: Little brother, little brother. It's only the custom. I have to be hard on you. That's how it's done. And what about debts? Do you owe money? Do you have any unfulfilled obligation on your conscience?

JOSÉ LUIS: I—I don't—

MARCELINA: Examine your heart, José Luis. Answer clearly.

JOSÉ LUIS: I don't owe money, not as far as I know.

VICENTE: (*wheeling around*) You mean you don't know? Atakáu! You come here after a wife and you don't know your own debts? Karahu! What do you think we are?

JOSÉ LUIS: (*sullenly*) I don't owe money.

VICENTE: Now, now. Don't take it wrong, Wayqíy. —And what about your labor obligations? Who can vouch for you? Nobody!

JOSÉ LUIS: Taytáy, you know that when I worked on the road here in Chiripata the people spoke well of me. I worked hard, I was dependable, I earned my salary.

VICENTE: As one speaks well of foxes! And what road are you making now? Where's your bulldozer? What's your salary?

JOSÉ LUIS: It wasn't my bulldozer. It belonged to the Ministry of Transportation. And I don't work on the road crew anymore. Adriana must have told you that. (*tries again unsuccessfully to catch Adriana's eye*) We had some bad luck . . .

VICENTE: Bad luck! So bad luck made you drink!

JOSÉ LUIS: (*upset*) Yes! Dios mio—

VICENTE: So here's our mighty bulldozer man, with no bulldozer and no salary. And you come asking for a wife, karahu! Then surely you're bringing us something else. Maybe you have land in Mayumarca—bean fields, corn fields?

JOSÉ LUIS: No, my brothers have it all. I'm not a comunero, and you know that, Taytáy. I never lived and worked the land in Mayumarca.

VICENTE: Then it must be animals!

MARCELINA: Llamas maybe!

VICENTE: That must be it! There are so many llamas in Mayumarca.

JOSÉ LUIS: (*exhausted*) Don't mock me, Taytáy.

VICENTE: Now, now, Wayqíy. It's only customary. I have to be
hard on you. Little brother, you come as a wandering
orphan to Chiripata asking for a wife. Asking to be
my son-in-law. Asking for my one little pigeon. You
know that here in Chiripata we divide our land and
animals among all our children, giving a fair share
to each one. And you know that Adriana is our only
child, so that she'll bring our whole livelihood to her
marriage. Now what can I say to a wandering orphan
boy who asks this of me—?

JOSÉ LUIS: Taytáy—

VICENTE: I can only think he's a thief in the night, with eyes for
everything I own.

MARCELINA: Atakáu!

(*José Luis again tries to catch Adriana's eye, to no avail; he
looks around desperately, looks down at his empty hands.*)

JOSÉ LUIS: (*sagging, in despair*) Then I'll go. Forgive me, Taytáy. I'll leave you alone. I'll leave you all alone.

(*He starts to rise; Adriana looks up in alarm, then averts her
eyes again. Vicente and Marcelina close in on José Luis;
Vicente puts his hand on the young man's shoulder.*)

VICENTE: Sit and rest, sit and rest, little brother.

MARCELINA: It's only the custom when you ask for a wife. The
soup will be ready soon.

(*José Luis sits again, exhausted and demoralized.*)

(*Dim light comes up on the Story Platform. In silhouette we
see the condor man standing in the cauldron with wings*)

*raised and outstretched. Steam begins to rise out of the caul-
dron.)*

VICENTE: If you take on such an obligation to me, I <u>have</u> to ask
what you'll give in return. But, don't worry, little
brother, we're kind-hearted people. I think we can
help you. Of course I can't let you take Adriana to
Cuzco. She doesn't want to live there. And what have
you got there? Nothing! What have you got in Mayumarca? Nothing! What have you got in Sicuani?
Worse than nothing! But here in Chiripata we have
everything—a house, land, animals, a wife, even a
road.

MARCELINA: Maybe we could build a new house right by the
road, where I have those bean fields.

VICENTE: Next year, or the year after, we could plant barley, or
maybe onions, to sell for money.

MARCELINA: You could set up a little store in the new house,
right there by the road. Selling candles, tragu,
kerosene . . .

VICENTE: *(trying to conceal his irony)* That's progress!
Progress in Chiripata!

JOSÉ LUIS: *(confused and overwhelmed)* What can I do? *(tries
to get up and go to Adriana)* I don't know what to
do . . .

VICENTE: Adriana! Ususíy! Come here! Tell us what you think
of this idea.

*(Adriana raises her head, revealing an expectant face. She
rises and approaches them, followed by Suzicha. The four
of them nearly enclose José Luis. He unsuccessfully reaches
for Adriana's hand.)*

ADRIANA: Father, yes! Maybe it's possible!

MARCELINA: A little modern store, right by the road . . .

*(On the Story Platform, a menacing red glow comes up
around the base of the cauldron. More steam begins to rise.
The condor man's wings tremble.)*

JOSÉ LUIS: *(to Adriana, subdued and desperate)* We should

talk this over—

ADRIANA: (*appearing not to hear him*) With an aluminum roof, instead of thatch! And a wooden floor.

SUZICHA: And maybe two stories high!

VICENTE: Well, little loved ones—then what shall we say to this wandering orphan boy? He doesn't even have coca and tragu to ask for a wife!

MARCELINA: Well, we have coca and tragu. He'll have to use ours.

VICENTE: He uses ours! To woo our daughter! Ay taytalláy! This is all backwards and upside down and inside out. But that's the way it is. Hinayá kashan. What else can we do?

(*Marcelina produces a large bag of coca and a large full bottle of tragu. She gives them to Vicente. Vicente carefully approaches José Luis, as if stalking him.*)

(*Light is slowly growing stronger on the Story Platform. More steam is rising. The condor man's wings are falling to his sides.*)

VICENTE: (*offering the coca and tragu to José Luis*) Friend, here is the coca and tragu you need if you want to ask for a wife. Don't worry that it's mine. You'll repay me later. I don't mind, dear brother, urpicháy. Go ahead.

(*José Luis dazedly stands up, glancing from Vicente to Adriana. He takes the coca and tragu.*)

(*On the Story Platform there is a sudden hiss and puff of steam. The condor man begins to slump; his wings tremble and droop.*)

JOSÉ LUIS: Thank you.

(*The family is triumphant. Marcelina throws back her head and laughs. Vicente puts his hand on José Luis's shoulder.*)

VICENTE: Hiyalli! Now you can ask for your wife! (*withdraws his hand*) But, my dear boy, you're still soaking wet! Marcelina, take off his wet jacket! Adriana! Get your husband some dry clothes!

(He presses José Luis back down onto the stool. The young man still looks dazed, places the coca and tragu on the floor. Adriana hurries to the clothes beam, and pulls down dead José's poncho. Suzicha produces a fancy ch'ullu from among the bed clothes. Marcelina firmly helps José Luis take off his jacket. Vicente walks over to the bedside and takes the poncho from Adriana. Again, he carefully approaches José Luis, as if stalking him.)

MARCELINA: Now for some warm clothes, dear boy. Real clothes!

(Vicente raises the poncho and puts it over José Luis's head. His gesture is reminiscent of a hunter bagging his prey, and also of the condor dance. Suzicha runs up behind José Luis and puts the ch'ullu on his head.)

(On the Story Platform, the condor man slumps yet further, his wings flopping over the sides of the cauldron. There is another hiss and billow of steam.)

(Leaning forward, Vicente takes José Luis by both elbows and raises him to his feet. For a moment the old man stands still, startled. Then he takes José Luis's shoulders in a formal embrace, with great feeling.)

VICENTE: José! José qatay! Son-in-law!

(He leads José Luis to the bench, presses him down, and stands over him victorious, holding the tragu and coca. Marcelina stands over him on the other side. Adriana's attention is taken up by Suzicha who clutches at her.)

VICENTE: <u>Now</u> we can celebrate. Now we can drink with the Mountain Lords, with Apu Mallku Tusuna!

(Vicente pours a shot and raises it to Apu Mallku Tusuna. Light fades on the house.)

(Light grows more intense on the Story Platform as it fades on the house. Steam billows and hisses. The condor man collapses into the cauldron with a muffled shriek. His black wings flop around in the steam.)

(Lights go out.)

The End

Ethnographic Notes and Comments

The notes that follow are meant to place *Condor Qatay* in the general context of rural Andean culture and to address some specific points that figure in the text. They cannot replace wider reading in Andean ethnography. Throughout these Notes and Comments we refer to a selection of basic works in English that should help enhance your understanding and enjoyment of *Condor Qatay*. The bibliographies of these books, in turn, should provide a fairly complete guide to further works in English and to the extensive and excellent literature available in Spanish.

THE SETTING

Chiripata is a fictional community. Through the play's dialogue one may infer that it is located in the southern Peruvian Department of Cuzco, Peru, high in the mountain tundra (*puna*) about 3500 meters in altitude. The city of Cuzco and town of Sicuani are real places, but the other smaller communities mentioned, such as Mayumarca and Misk'i-unu, are fictional. Mallku Tusuna is a fictional mountain. In producing *Condor Qatay*, it would be possible to change the setting and relocate Chiripata to any fairly remote, high-altitude locale in the Peruvian, Bolivian, or Ecuadorean Andes. Such a move would require certain adjustments and involve the collaboration of someone knowledgeable about the geography, culture, and language of the region in question. (In fact this might be an interesting exercise for students of Andean ethnography.) Every effort would have to be made to avoid mixing regional styles. While the tale of the condor son-in-law and the social processes explored in the play are found throughout the Andes, there is a great deal of variation in regional styles of dress, dance, coca-chewing etiquette, and language. Many of the Quechua phrases, like "riki" and "urpicháy," are specific to Cuzco; appropriate regional variants would have to be substituted to accommodate a change in setting. Obviously, different towns would have to be substituted for Sicuani and Cuzco.

Our play is set in a precipitous mountain landscape where local ecology varies with altitude. This "vertical ecology" has ramifications in almost every aspect of rural life (see Murra's classic article, "Rite and Crop in the Inca State," 1973, and Brush's *Mountain, Field and Family,* 1977; also see Bastien 1978; Flores Ochoa 1979; Isbell 1978; Murra, Wachtel, and Revel 1986; Orlove 1977). For millennia the high puna regions, whose subsistence is limited to potato cultivation and the herding of native camelids, have been connected through trading and kinship with valley communities in order to exchange potatoes and wool for lower altitude products like corn, chili peppers, and coca. In a community like Chiripata, most households would have kinsmen or *compadres* (see Glossary) in valley communities, and many of the men would travel occasionally to the upper reaches of the rain forest to work on coca plantations. Men would also travel during slack periods in the agricultural cycle to work as porters or as construction workers in cities like Cuzco. As a source on these travels we highly recommend *Andean Lives: Gregorio Condori Mamani and Asunta Quispe Huamán*, an autobiography of a Cuzco street porter and his wife, translated and edited by Gelles and Martinez Escobar (1996).

Agricultural fields in the Cuzco region of Peru. The small, scattered holdings help minimize the effects of hailstorms and maximize access to different micro-environments.

We conceive of Chiripata as an independent community, never incorporated into one of the neo-feudal landed estates called *haciendas*. Communities of this type often protected their independence by assuming the kind of cultural conservatism exemplified in the play by Vicente. Although the hacienda system was abolished during President Velasco's agrarian reform of the 1970s, its heritage is still strongly felt in the Peruvian countryside. (The many good sources on the Andean hacienda system include the novels of José María Arguedas; as well as Jackson 1994; Klein 1983; Skar 1982; Smith 1989; Spalding 1984; and the anthologies edited by Orlove and Custred 1980; Poole 1994; and Starn, DeGregori and Kirk 1995.)

WORLDVIEW

Throughout *Condor Qatay*, the characters orient themselves spatially and emotionally with reference to landmarks, particularly their primary sacred mountain, Mallku Tusuna. Like many other Andean people, inhabitants of Chiripata experience the landscape as alive and powerful. The Earth as a whole is felt to be alive, and every landmark—from snow-capped peaks to rock outcrops and lakes—possesses a name and individual personality. The Quechua word *pacha*, which means "world," may refer both to the physical earth and to a very specific moment in time. Each pacha has a specific sun, with its own quality of light. Andean beliefs and practices concerning this animate universe co-exist, and to some extent have blended, with Catholic beliefs and ritual forms. (This theme is treated at length in Allen 1988; moreover, Bastien 1978; Dover 1992; Gose 1994; Isbell 1978; and Sallnow 1987 also provide good treatments of this theme.) Urton (1981) provides a fine synthesis of cosmological beliefs as does Salomon in his introduction to the English translation of *The Hua-rochiri Manuscript* (Salomon and Urioste 1991). MacCormack (1991) and Silverblatt (1987) provide excellent source

In a rural community in southern Peru, a chapel stands next to a road completed in the early 1980s.

St. John's Eve. A couple and their eldest son (far left) share coca and *tragu* while the younger children suck on hard candies.

material on cosmological beliefs during the Inca and Colonial periods.

The landscape arouses emotional and intellectual interests due to the animation and power *runakuna* (Quechua-speaking people) feel in the places themselves. Sacred Places are felt to watch over all human activity. Sickness, poverty, and bad luck are attributed to their wrath, just as prosperity and health are seen as signs of their favor. Throughout Peru and Bolivia, the coca leaf plays an important role in this cosmological system. Like the humming top and the lightning flash, it brings different states and dimensions of existence into communication with each other. The ritual blowing of coca leaves, called *phukuy* (pronounced "pooh-kwee"), is the most basic religious duty and the essence of all other ritual. It is through coca leaves that rural Andeans relate to the Sacred Places among which they live. In phukuy the animating essence of the leaves, called *sami*, is sent to the Earth and Sacred Places. Coca's sami is manifested through its energizing and medicinal qualities. The coca chewer utters an invocation in order to direct the sami to its recipient—for example, to a specific Mountain Lord (*Apu*) known to control the weather, or to the ancestral "Grandfathers" (*Machula Aulanchis*) who control crop fertility. Phukuy is performed in a perfunctory way during the daily routine, but when important matters are at hand—as when Vicente waits for José Luis toward the end of act II—it must be sent with great concentration and strength of mind. (For discussions of coca's physiological effects, its relationship to cultural identity in the Andes, and its relationship to cocaine and the narcotics trade, see Allen 1988; Morales 1989; and Pacini and Franquemont 1986.)

Ritual specialists use coca leaves to divine the future, to learn of distant events, or to find lost objects. In *Condor Qatay*, Inocencia "reads" the leaves to inquire after the welfare of absent Adriana. Scene 8 portrays the divination ritual as it would be carried out in the Department of Cuzco. With the phrase *tawa iskina* ("four corners"), Inocencia pours libations of alcohol on a cloth, defining it as a kind of miniature quadripartite cosmos. As she drops the coca leaves onto the cloth, she calls to the Sacred Places, *Sut'ita willaway!* ("Tell me clearly!"). The Places then make the leaves fall into a configuration that—properly interpreted—reflects events in the real world. (Coca divination is discussed in many sources, including Allen 1988; Bastien 1978, 1987; and Sharon 1978.)

Inocencia tells Vicente and Marcelina to "feed" Apu Mallku Tusuna with a *dispachu*, to obtain the mountain's favor. The dispachu is a bundle composed of coca leaves and other ingredients such as seeds and fat. All these ingredients fall under the generic term *hampi* (medicine), which in its most basic sense refers to any energizing substance that helps remedy an imbalance in some part of the cosmos. Bastien's *Healers of the Andes* (1987) provides a good analysis of indigenous theories of health and disease. (For background on health and nutrition in Andean communities, see Bastien and Donahue 1981; Baker and Little 1976.)

ETHNICITY, KINSHIP, AND THE AMBIGUITY OF THE CONDOR

Birds serve as intermediaries between human beings and Sacred Places. The hummingbird, whose wings move faster than the eye can see, is thought to be an emissary of the Apus and a messenger from the dead; the condor is the Mountain Lords' most powerful representative and confidant.

Films are the best source of information on the role of the condor in Andean thought and ritual. The ethnographic films *Our God the Condor* and *The Condor and the Bull* explore the revival of the Yawar Fiesta or Feast of Blood (the subject of Vicente and Cipriano's conversation in scene 4). These films follow the condor as it is trapped, tethered to a bull, made to fight, and finally released, showing very clearly how the great bird is loved, revered, and victimized. A NOVA television special, *Shadow of the Condor*, also includes some material on the condor's cultural significance.

Beautiful in flight and ugly on the ground, the mighty carrion-eating condor is venerated and feared, admired and loathed. The condor's role in traditional folklore is similarly ambiguous. Like myths and folktales everywhere, the story of Condor Qatay explores contradictions inherent in people's lives; it is a study in paradox which explores the interrelated issues of *ethnicity* and *kinship* in rural Andean life.

ETHNICITY

The connection with Sacred Places is an essential aspect of native Andean (*runa*) identity. In one way or another, it is the bond between a group of people and Sacred Places that creates an *ayllu* (community; see Glossary). Depending on their moods, Sacred Places may be protective or ruthlessly destructive; rural Andeans approach them with a sense of familiarity and gratitude mixed with caution and distrust. Because they are fickle sources of wealth and power, Sacred Places are felt to resemble mestizos, particularly the *hacendados* (land-lords) who until recently dominated many indigenous communities. This is where the paradox lies: Sacred Places provide a basic grounding for runa identity, and yet they are experienced as like *misti* (mestizo) landowners, the runa's antithesis. (See Gose 1994; also, Nash 1979 provides an interesting analysis of these contradictions in the context of Bolivian tin miners.)

What is a mestizo? The question is not easy to answer. The categories "Indian" and "mestizo" ostensibly refer to a racial distinction between pure-blooded Native Americans and people with a mixed Native American and Spanish ancestry. However, this distinction is illusory; the racial idiom is used in reference to cultural differences. Genetically speaking, the whole highland population is of fairly uniform mixed ancestry. The difference between mestizo and Indian, or *misti* and *runa* in Quechua, is that of cultural style and ethnic affiliation. To be mestizo is to be oriented toward one's European heritage, be bilingual in Spanish and Quechua, participate as shopkeepers and truck drivers in the national money economy, and wear factory-made, western-style clothing. Mestizo religion is Roman Catholicism, with some conversion to Evangelical Protestantism. To be Indian, or runa, is to speak Quechua, to continue to live in ayllus, to chew coca leaves, and to wear *runa p'acha*, or traditional woven clothing. Subsistence agriculture and barter play a large role in runa household economies; if they traffic as intermediaries it is on a very small scale. While Catholic, their religious life includes a strong Native American connection with Mother Earth and the sacred landscape. (For further discussion of ethnicity in the Andean highlands see Núñez del Prado 1973; Van den Berghe 1977; Rasnake 1988; and Weismantel 1988; see also the anthologies edited by Orlove and Custred 1980; Whitten 1981; Poole 1994; and Starn, DeGregori, and Kirk 1995.)

However, this description does not capture the complexity of the misti/runa distinction. It is important to understand that mestizos and Indians really are not two groups of people; the distinction is a conceptual one, an opposition between two opposed yet interdependent ways of life. While the misti/runa distinction is rigid in concept, it tends to be fluid in practice.

Runa p'acha. A couple in the province of Paucartambo, Peru stands in their traditional dress.

A single individual can signal his movement back and forth between the two social codes by changing his language, clothing, and deportment—alternately defining himself or herself as runa or as misti according to the way of life he or she chooses to adopt. This kind of code-switching, while situationally convenient, may set up a state of inner tension and ambivalence, especially in young adults like José Luis and Adriana. In many ways our play is about this conflict. It finds an apt vehicle in the condor, who contains a similar inner tension between his identity as sacred representative of the Mountain Lords and as predatory mestizo outsider.

The condor qatay appears to the young woman and her family as an elegantly dressed mestizo merchant; in other tales the condor is likened to a lawyer or a priest. Like the condor, merchants, lawyers, and priests are experienced as fascinating, powerful, and untrustworthy figures. The disagreeable "otherness" of these figures is expressed by the condor's trait of carrion-eating, while his majestic flight and huge size express their glamour and menace. In the folktale, the Indian family members are victimized by the condor. The opposition between them is resolved violently when they in turn victimize the condor, who is himself cooked and eaten like a chicken. The condor's final nakedness, emphasized in any telling of the story, evokes a phrase used in many parts of the Andean highlands to describe mestizos—qalakuna, "the naked ones" (Isbell 1978).

KINSHIP AND MARRIAGE

Andean ayllus are composed of a network of households linked through ties of blood, marriage and compadrazgo (godparenthood; see Glossary). Relatives through marriage (affines) rely heavily on each other in a tense bond of mutual dependence and obligation. An enduring alliance between a man and woman is recognized within the ayllu as a marriage even if—as often happens—the couple waits several years before passing through a religious or civil marriage ceremony.

When Vicente refers to José Luis as Adriana's "husband" in scene 13, he is indirectly expressing acceptance of the relationship. (Good discussions of Andean kinship in English are found in Bolton and Mayer 1977; Skar 1982; and Isbell 1978; also see chapter three in Allen 1988.)

Some of the most fundamental links in the ayllu network are formed through the relationship between men and their *qatays*. (The term *qatay* may refer to either daughter's husband or wife's brother; however, the brother-in-law relationship does not figure in the play.) The ancient tale of the condor qatay continues to capture the depth and conflict of this basic economic, social, and emotional bond. The condor son-in-law is predator, interloper, and victim; he is consumed in the end by his wife's family.

Turning to our play, we find an aging couple (Vicente and Marcelina) living with their widowed daughter (Adriana) and her child. Adriana's deceased husband (José) had lived with his wife's parents, and they had expected him to support them in their old age. This is an example of uxorilocal residence, in which a man comes to live with his wife's family. Uxorilocality is not considered the ideal situation in Andean communities; couples prefer to set up their own households (neolocality) or to move in with the husband's parents (virilocality). Nevertheless, uxorilocality has existed in Andean ayllus for centuries, serving as a crucial mechanism through which an ayllu with a shortage of men can recruit new male members.

This is what we see happening in *Condor Qatay*. In Chiripata, as in most Andean ayllus, inheritance is cognatic, meaning that children of both sexes receive inheritance from both their parents. (Some regions, however, retain a pre-Columbian pattern in which females inherit from their mothers and males from their fathers.) When children in these communities come of age and marry, each receives a share of his or her parents' herds and use-rights to land. Newlyweds tend to live for a time with one set of parents (usually the grooms') before they establish their own household. Generally the youngest remains to care for the parents in their old age, in return receiving their house and remaining animals and land. Of all the offspring, this youngest child is likely to gain the largest inheritance. Thus, a man with little to inherit may be attracted by marriage to the youngest daughter of relatively prosperous parents even though it means living with his in-laws. In this way an outsider with no inheritance whatsoever may gain a foothold in the ayllu. He will come as a qatay to live in his father-in-law's house, accepting his subservient position in the knowledge that eventually he, or his children, will take over the older man's status and property. The price he pays in prestige and independence may be heavy. One message in the condor qatay folktale is that an in-marrying son-in-law—even a rich mestizo possessed of supernatural powers—ultimately gives himself up to his wife's family.

Ideally a couple has several children, and the marriages of these children provide a group of sons-in-law and daughters-in-law to help them in their old age. In the play, Vicente and Marcelina have only Adriana, their one surviving child, to care for them. They depend on her to bring home a husband both to provide a kind of social security, and to renew their household for another generation. Their problem is, on the one hand, to find a man whom Adriana likes enough to marry and, on the other, who is willing to be consumed by their need for him.

COMMUNICATION IN SPEECH AND GESTURE

The inhabitants of Chiripata speak Quechua, once the dominant administrative language of the Inca Empire. Quechua actually comprises a family of languages spoken throughout Andean South America from southern Colombia to northern Argentina. Approximately twelve million people speak languages of the Quechua family, and about eight million of these people are bilingual in Quechua and Spanish. Among bilinguals, Quechua is generally the language of the home and intimacy while Spanish is the language of commerce and law. Even among fellow Quechua speakers, bilinguals sometimes slip in and out of Spanish, as José Luis does in scene 3.

Quechua is almost exclusively an oral language. The Incas encoded information and ideas, not in alphabetic writing, but in complex knotted strings called *quipus*. Later, the development of written Quechua was suppressed in its incipient stages after the Tupac Amaru Rebellion of 1780. Quechua has incorporated quite a lot of Spanish vocabulary in the five hundred years since the Spanish Conquest (for example, *siguru* from Spanish *seguro*; *yusulpayki* from Spanish *dios se le pague*). Nevertheless, the grammar has been little affected. Like many other Native American languages, Quechua is characterized by agglutination; phrases are formed by piling suffixes onto a root. For example, from *wasi* (house) and *riy* (to go), we can build the phrase, "Wasichayta ripushani" or "I am going away to my little house." The construction would look like this: *wasi*(house)-*cha*(little)-*y*(my)-*ta*(to) *ri*(go)-*pu*(out)-*sha* (present progressive)-*ni*(first person singular).

The first chapter of Mannheim's *The Language of the Inka since the Spanish Invasion* (1991) gives a good overview of Quechua linguistics. Other good sources include *South American Indian Languages: Retrospect and Prospect* edited by Klein and Stark (1985), and *Language in the Andes* edited by Cole, Hermon, and Martin (1994). Wright (1989) has published a traveller's phrase book for English speakers; for Quechua grammar, students may turn to textbooks by Morato-Peña (1995) and Soto-Ruíz (1993). On the relationship between Quechua poetry and culture, see Harrison (1989).

Quechua speakers delight in subtle linguistic embellishments, especially the use of diminutives and alliteration (e.g., the humorous nickname, Wayna Wanka). We have tried to convey a sense of this in the English text. (In scene 2, for example, "I can't fix those workers the same old thing every day. Would you just look in that sack for me?") The invocations and laments in *Condor Qatay* try to convey Quechua poetic forms, particularly through the use of parallelism.

Quechua speakers tend to be formal in their interactions. Greetings, partings, and thank-yous may be long and stylized, especially among older people, consistent with an underlying tendency to ritually mark boundaries of all kinds. The moments when individuals separate or encounter each other are signalled as significant through elaborate litanies of thanks and reassurance. Similarly, at the moment day passes into night—when the candle is lit and the door of the house is

Serving *tragu* during a house-raising party.

closed—everyone in the house greets each other anew (as in scenes 2 and 8). The litanies of farewell and thank-you provide great opportunities for rhetorical virtuosity and oneupman-ship. In scene 5, Vicente employs this strategy to put young José Luis in his place, making typical use of Quechua irony and indirection.

Communication is often indirect; individuals prefer not to risk open hostility by putting their companions on the spot. For example, in scene 4 Cipriano lets Vicente know that José Luis is visiting his daughter and yet accepts Vicente's denial of the possibility. Another aspect of indirection is the avoid-ance of eye contact. Young women in particular avoid looking at men; thus Adriana averts her head during most of the con-versations between Vicente and José Luis in scenes 5 and 13.

The lamentation of Marcelina and Vicente (scene 8) is among the most difficult passages in the play. The two laments should be delivered simultaneously (Marcelina starting in a few moments after Vicente) but not in unison and without the actors establishing eye contact. They each seem to be in their own world; only toward the end, as their lamentation reaches its highest emotional pitch, should they begin to speak more in concert. Marcelina should cry in a high, almost falsetto, voice.

Ethnographic films are a good source of information about Andean "body language." They should be used carefully, how-ever, to avoid superficial imitation and caricature. We have found that films are best used after students have done quite a lot of reading and improvisation on their own. Basic infor-mation about typical postures and mannerisms can be learned from film, but the walk and carriage so characteristic of Andean people are more likely to come through the experi-ence of carrying loads on the back and paying careful attention to the demands put on one's body while climbing steep inclines. Physically speaking, the most difficult posture for North Americans is "sitting"; this is actually a stable, squatting position with feet close together and flat on the floor. Women in particular spend much of their time in this position, and men sit this way when nothing else is available.

Dance and Music

In scene 11 Vicente is overcome with joy at the return of his daughter and exclaims: "Let's dance! Let's make Carnival! Let's wake up the ayllu and tell them Adriana's home!" The aging and tired grandfather spontaneously turns to music and dance to express himself. In communities like Chiripata, dancing to the sounds of flutes and drums, brass instruments and—increasingly—recorded music is a part of both the simplest rituals and the most elaborate festivals.

In our classes we use both music and dance to involve our students in exercises and improvisations. In one extended meditation exercise the student listens mentally to the song of his/her place and begins to sing with it. This exercise often

Dancers "wake up the hills" on St. John's Day (June 24).

culminates with the entire group coming together to form a community song, and occasionally leads to spontaneous dancing. In another exercise, students use notebooks and pencils as drums and drumsticks, tapping along to the complex rhythms of Andean music. After the music is turned off, they find their own rhythms and then begin to communicate with each other and develop group rhythms. This exercise might be good training for the lamentation scene discussed earlier. The first half of John Cohen's film *Carnival in Q'eros* very effectively explores this aspect of communal music-making in Andean communities; as in the lament, each individual begins independently but gradually moves toward a musical consensus with the group.

Early on in the play (scene 2) music and dance are incorporated into Marcelina's storytelling, as the mestizo youth impresses the young woman with his flute playing. Their teasing banter turns into a dance as they circle one another to the sounds of a drum and flute *waynu* (dance/song) typical of the most traditional indigenous communities. Gradually this gives way to a mestizo version of the waynu accompanied by guitars and mandolin or brass instruments; the youth transforms himself back into a condor, sweeps up the young woman, and flies away with her. The transformation of the waynu, both musically and choreographically, expresses the young woman's attraction to the ways of the mestizo youth. She is drawn away from her runa orientation and towards his way of life. As the story scenes mirror the action of the rest of the play, so too, this dance mirrors the teasing courtship between José Luis and Adriana in scene 3, as the two circle each other tossing stones and slapping at each other's legs with switches (on courtship see Millones and Pratt 1990).

In the condor dance of scene 6 the condors devour a raw carcass, while at the same time initiating the young woman into their world. The dance begins with the condors flapping their wings rhythmically and circling a large piece of animal carcass which they soon tear into bloody chunks and eat voraciously. Finally, the condor man tears away a piece to present to his bride. The dance comes to an abrupt halt as she rejects it completely, refusing to be included in the condor community. In the final story scene, the condor man is duped into the boiling cauldron while the young woman's family dances around it, forcing him back into the steaming water when he tries to escape. Their aggressively celebratory dance is reminiscent of the condor dance in which circling the carcass is the dominant movement.

Ideally, an imaginative choreographer should thoroughly research the dances of the Cuzco area before creating the work. Films about the condor, like those mentioned earlier, provide some insight into the kind of movement required in the condor dance. John Cohen's film *Dancing with the Incas* includes some footage of a condor dance, illustrating the basic idea we have in mind. His films *Mountain Music of Peru* and *Carnival in Q'eros* provide many good illustrations of the full spectrum of music and dance in the Andes.

Music can be used very effectively to establish the play's mood and bring an audience into the Andean world. Before the performance begins, and during the transitions between the scenes, music not only fills the darkened silences but carries an audience from the mood of one scene into that of the next. All of the music in *Condor Qatay* could be created by live musicians if time and resources permit. Recordings, available in many stores, may be used as well. Titles such as *Mountain Music of Peru* (Smithsonian Folkways Recordings) may serve as a starting point for choosing appropriate music. We suggest using music actually recorded in Andean communities, while avoiding professional recordings of music composed for Euro-American sensibilities. *Huayno Music of Peru*, collected by John Cohen for Discos IEMPSA and Arhoolie Productions, Inc., is a good source of mestizo waynus.

The sound of the zumbayllu spinning may be recorded electronically or suggested by appropriate flute music. The important thing is that the sound convey the feeling of the moment, the spirit if you will. The right zumbayllu will dance appropriately without the aid of a choreographer.

Afterword
The Zumbayllu and Experiential Learning

This last section will look at one small element in the play—
the top or *zumbayllu*—and its relationship to the kind of work
we have been doing with our students.

The top took on an important role during our first semester
of teaching together, when we decided to use images from
Arguedas's *Deep Rivers* in some of our meditation exercises.
Deep Rivers is itself a meditative, introspective and yet very
imagistic book, and we asked students which images they
found strongest in order to use their suggestions to focus the
meditation exercises. A number of students chose the zumbayllu as the strongest image. The zumbayllu turned out to
work particularly well in meditation exercises; the spinning
image (as well as the humming sound it evokes in—what shall
we call it!—the mind's ear?) seems to have a mantra-like effect
that concentrates the thoughts.

Suzicha (Jen Deitch) plays with her top as her grandmother (Melissa Foulger) spins thread. *Photo by Ken Cobb.*

In our class we draw on the students' previous experience of spinning tops, but we ask them to contextualize the experience in a new way, following Arguedas's lead. In *Deep Rivers*, spinning the top teaches the boy Ernesto that all matter is potentially animate, and that rapid movement, light, and sound have powers to open lines of communication with Mountain Lords, rivers, and distant relatives. ("How could you fashion a toy to make it change its voice like that?" asks a priest in the book. "No, Brother, it wasn't me, it's the material it's made of," replies the boy [p. 117]). When spinning, the little wooden top becomes a fantastic animal with a single "paw" and four "eyes." The eyes sing; the top is a bearer of messages.

The central chapter of Arguedas's book, the sixth out of eleven, is called "Zumbayllu." Arguedas begins it with an ethnographic discourse on the ending -*yllu*. He wants to be sure we realize that this child's toy is related to a complex of culturally significant ideas:

> The Quechua ending *yllu* is onomatopoeic. *Yllu* in one form, means the music of tiny wings in flight, music created by the movement of light objects. This term is similar to another broader one—*illa*. *Illa* is the name used for a certain kind of light, also for monsters with birth defects caused by moonbeams. . . . All *illas* bring good or bad luck, always to the nth degree. To touch an *illa* and to either die or be resurrected, is possible. (1978:64)

Arguedas relates the zumbayllu to the scissors dancers, and to the *pinkuyllu* (the great deep-voiced flute).

> . . . The voice of the *pinkuyllu* . . . dazzles and exalts the Indians, unleashing their strength; while listening to it, they defy death . . . they dance unceasingly . . . no probe, music or element can penetrate deeper into the human heart. . . . The suffix *yllu* signifies the diffusion of this kind of music . . . (1978:66)

The zumbayllu has the same effect on Ernesto:

> The song of the top penetrated deep into my ear, reviving memories of rivers, and of the black trees that overhang the walls of the abysses. . . . What similarity was there, what current flowed between the world of the deep valleys and the body of that little mobile toy . . . ? (1978:68)

Ernesto asks Antero, the zumbayllu's owner, to give him the toy; in return Antero asks him to ghost-write love letters to his girlfriend: love letters for a zumbayllu, good Andean *ayni* (equivalent exchange). Thinking of the zumbayllu, Ernesto

starts to write and begins to imagine himself as a hummingbird (messenger of the Mountain Lords) carrying his message,
not to Antero's girlfriend, but to the Quechua-speaking village
girl he himself loves.

In this chapter we are drawn into a web of associations, into
"the imaginative universe in which their acts are signs" (Geertz
1973:13). Following this up in class, we ask the students to
describe their imagined zumbayllus. We ask about their zumbayllus' songs. As part of their meditation, with closed eyes,
we ask them to hum the songs; through the sound each con-
nects with the voices of the other students. In other medita-
tions they have created a mental landscape, and we have them
use the zumbayllu to communicate with the Places in this
landscape. We have never laid out a didactic interpretation of
the zumbayllu for the students, as we are doing now. Rather,
we encourage them to use Arguedas's imagery to fashion their
own zumbayllus in their imaginations. This personal zumbayllu is drawn from their own experience but is situated—made
meaningful—in a culturally new way.

This meditation work is done during the first few weeks of
the semester. We soon turn to the content of the ethnographic
readings, and work toward creating our scenarios. The first
step is to learn and practice some of the little indispensable
ceremonies of everyday life—greeting, parting, serving and
accepting food, sharing coca leaves.

The connection with the meditation work comes through
the web of culturally determined associations into which the
zumbayllu has drawn us, and is particularly important as students learn the ceremony surrounding coca chewing. The
strong parallel between the cultural meaning of coca leaves
and Ernesto's relationship to the zumbayllu is particularly
clear in this passage:

> "If I make it spin and blow its song in the direction of Chall-
> huanca, will it reach my father's ears?" I asked Markask'a.

> "It will brother! Distance doesn't mean anything to it. . . .
> First you speak to it, into one of its eyes, giving it your mes-
> sage and telling it which way to go. And then, when it's singing,
> you blow, you blow it carefully in the direction you want it to
> go, and keep on giving it your message. And the zumbayllu will

sing into the ear of whoever is expecting you." (Arguedas 1978:117–118)

This passage reminded Catherine Allen of being taught how to chew coca leaves. For the coca phukuy to be effective it should be sent with the same intensity of involvement that Ernesto felt for his zumbayllu. Its performance is premised on this understanding of coca as a kind of cosmic transmitter.

The purpose of our zumbayllu exercises is to prepare the students to perform the ceremony of coca chewing not as empty gestures, but with the totality of the event in mind. There is an abstractness in the ideas involved in coca chewing, and a distance from the students' experience, which make it difficult to introduce directly. In contrast, the spinning top is a vivid and familiar image which can lead students into a different thought-world. To make the transition we have the students reprise the zumbayllu exercises, replacing the top and its song with the coca leaves.

Coca chewing is an adult activity. Children grow into coca chewing as they grow into other adult activities, like spinning and weaving, cultivating the fields, and caring for herds of animals. Each of these activities has a patron saint, and as a person slowly learns the requisite skills through practice, she or he is said to become *santuyuq*, "endowed with the attributes of the saint." With these skills mastered, a person can participate in the network of reciprocal exchange (*ayni*) that structures rural Andean society. Children at play are beginning to acquire, or absorb, these skills necessary for adult life.

Playing with the top helps prepare Ernesto for his adult life. As we approach the end of the novel the boy is caught up, first, in a revolt at a nearby hacienda and afterwards, in a typhoid epidemic. The zumbayllu appears less and less frequently. Finally he buries it (a significant and not altogether negative action in an Andean context). Although he longs to play with it again, he is sidetracked by adult crises. He comes upon the Idiot Woman gravely ill and instead of playing with his toy he attends her in death.

Condor Qatay uses the zumbayllu as a framing device, to help draw the audience into the Andes. As the play begins, Suzicha plays with the top while her grandmother spins. The top's

Adult activities. A woman weaves at a horizontal back-strap loom, *above; opposite page,* a man fashions a grass rope to lash a new thatch roof on his house. Female tasks are properly horizontal while male ones are vertical.

hum is the first sound in the play, and the distant condor on the mountaintop listens and spreads his wings in response.

And, much as in our class, the transition from top-spinning to thread-spinning expresses Suzicha's development from child to incipient adulthood. Spinning thread is a basic cultural, transformative activity—similar to spinning the top, but with an adult purpose.

It was surprising to realize how closely our students' learning process paralleled that of Ernesto in *Deep Rivers*. In a sense, we stumbled upon the zumbayllu and kept using it because it works for the class. It works because it leads the students from the open and decontextualized condition of childhood play into a new way of relating to the world; this becomes the basis for learning culturally defined modes of interaction. Of course, it does this with nothing like the depth of real childhood experience—but for the students who "get it" (and some of them do), the underlying process is very similar.

It is in performance—in the actual doing—that we learn with our bodies as well as our minds. Gregory Bateson (e.g., 1972) liked to say that the deepest learning sinks to automatic pre-articulated levels, it is felt, and becomes habitual. This is similar to what Paul Connerton (1989) says about "how societies remember." People embody their cultures—that is, they learn a way of being in the world which they express with

A twelve-year-old shepherd girl pauses on her way home from the pasture. Her baby brother peers out from the bundle on her back.

words, organizations, and artifacts, but first and foremost with their bodies. With mindful bodies and embodied minds, we learn whatever it is we truly know.

In the introduction we commented that the actors' best preparation for this play will be an immersion in ethnographic literature and film, accompanied by improvisation and meditation exercises. Even with this preparation, the results will be an approximation. It would be foolish to think that North American actors can, as it were, "become" Andean. Nevertheless, whatever its end product, the process of experiential learning is valuable because it impels the whole self to explore a different way of being in the world. This helps us experience our basic humanness as a vast (but not limitless) field of potentiality, in which many scenarios are possible. The scenarios differ according to the place and time in which they are played out. We are each drawn in touch with our own self as one such unfolding scenario, not unlike the other selves playing themselves out in manifold ways on other stages.

Glossary of Quechua Words

For most words, emphasis is placed on the next-to-the-last syllable. In exceptions, emphasis is indicated with an accent mark, as in "Achacháu!" (AchaCHAU!).

VOWELS

Quechua includes only three vowels, **a, i** and **u**. **A** is pronounced like the **a** in **a**but and the **o** in c**o**llect. **I** is pronounced like the **ee** in str**ee**t. **U** is pronounced like the **oo** in p**oo**l.

CONSONANTS

There are many consonants, including glottalized and aspirated varieties that will be unfamiliar to English speakers. In glottalized consonants (**ch', k', p', q', t'**) the air is stopped briefly, giving the consonant a somewhat explosive character.

125

Aspiration is indicated by an h after the consonant (**chh, kh, ph, qh, th**) and involves letting out a little puff of air that softens the consonant slightly. (Note that **ph** is closer to English **p** than to English **f**. Thus **phukuy** is pronounced **pooh-kwee**.)

Y at the beginning of a word is pronounced like the **y** in **y**ou. At the end of a word **y** changes the preceding vowel: **-ay** is pronounced like long **i** in site; **-iy** is pronounced like the **y** in eas**y**; **-uy** is pronounced rather like French **oui**.

A

Achacháu!   My goodness! Wow!
Achakaláu!   What a shame!
Achakaláy!   What a shame!
Achakáu!   How awful!
Adicha   diminutive of Adriana
Adicháy   My little Adicha (direct address—speaking to her)
Alaláu!   How cold! I'm freezing!
Allillanchu?   How are you? (lit., Is everything just fine?)
Allillanmi   I'm just fine.
Allinllaña   Good-bye!
allinmi   good, fine
Amayá!   Don't!
Añañáu!   How good! Yum!
apu   lord, usually refers to the Mountain Lords
Apu Mallku Tusuna   in the play, major Mountain Lord for the community of Chiripata
Apuriy!   Hurry up!
arí   yes
aula   grandmother (from Spanish, *abuela*)
Auláy   My Grandmother (direct address)
Aumarya   an old-fashioned greeting (from Spanish, *Ave María*)
ay!   Oh! Alas!
ayllu   a type of community indigenous to the Andes, based on ties of kinship and a common focus on Sacred Places often conceived of as ancestral
ayllu runa   an indigenous person from an ayllu

B

Buenas noches   (Spanish) Good evening.
Buenas tardes   (Spanish) Good afternoon.

C

-cha   diminutive suffix
chaki taqlla   Andean foot plow with a foot rest and sharp blade (chaki=foot; taqlla=plow)
Chaymantarí?   And what happened next?
chiri   cold
Chiripata   name of Adriana's community (lit., cold place)
cholo   a social type, transitional between Indian and mestizo; sometimes used as an insult, sometimes as an endearment
-chu   interrogative suffix (like a verbal question mark)
chullo   knitted cap with ear flaps, used by men
comadre   (Spanish) godmother, or the godmother of one's children. See *compadre*.
compadre   (Spanish) godfather, or the godfather of one's children; one of the strongest social bonds
comunero   (Spanish) member of an indigenous agricultural community

Ch'

ch'uñu   freeze-dried potatoes, prepared by a process of alternate freezing and thawing
ch'uspa   a small woven bag, used by men for carrying coca leaves

D

dispachu   offering bundle given to the Mother Earth, Mountain Lords, and Ancestors; usually burned, sometimes buried; from Spanish *despacho*
diuspagarasunki   a very polite way of saying thank-you; from Spanish, *Dios se le pagará* (God will pay you), combined with the Quechua interactive suffix, *-sunki*, indicating action from the 3rd to the 2nd person, i.e., "from him to you"

G

gracias   (Spanish) thank-you

H

Haku!   Let's go!
Hallpakusunchis   Let us chew coca together.
Hampu!   Come on in!
hamusayki   I'm coming to you
hamusaykiman   I want to come to you
hamushan   he, she, or it is coming
Hamuway!   Come to me! (imperative, direct command)
Hananáu!   I'm so tired!
hawa   grandchild
Hawachalláy   My dear little Grandchild (direct address)
Hawáy   My Grandchild (direct address)
hina   like this, like that, like so
hinallatapis   you're welcome
Hinayá   That's just the way it is.

I

Imaynallan?   How are you?
iskina   corner (from Spanish, *esquina*)

K

Karahu!   Damn! (from Spanish, *Caramba!*)
Karáy!   variant of Karahu!
kashan (kay)   it is (infinitive *kay*, to be)
kasqa   was, must have been
khuchi   pig
-ku   polite suffix (also reflexive)
kukuchi   damned soul, like a zombie

K'

k'ayra   frog
k'intu   a small offering of coca leaves

L

listu   ready (from Spanish, *listo*)
listullaña   all ready now!

LL (pronounced ly)

-lla an untranslatable suffix; gives the word an endearing, positive emphasis
llushkha muddy, slippery
llushkhallaña really slippery

M

machu old (not to be confused with Spanish, *macho*)
Machukuna Old Ones, Ancestors of the community
machula little old man, grandfather
Machula Aulanchis endearing term for the Ancestors
Machuláy My Grandpa (direct address)
maki hand
mallku young male bird; sometimes refers to condors
mama mother
Mamáy My Mother (direct address)
mamitay (mamítay) my mommy (Quechua *mama* combined with Spanish diminutive, *-ita*, plus first person possessive *-y*)
Mamitáy Mommy (direct address)
manachu samuwaq? don't you want to rest?
manan no
manan allinchu no good, bad
manaraq not yet
maqt'a adolescent boy, kid, guy
maway papa early potatoes
mihukuy please eat
misti mestizo, non-runa (from Spanish, *mestizo*)
montera (Spanish) flat fringed hat worn by women
muhu seed; *papa muhu*, small potatoes used as seed

Ñ (pronounced ny-)

ñachu? ready yet?
ñawin eye

P

pacha earth
Pacha Mama Mother Earth
pallay punchu fancy poncho, with complex designs

pana   sister of a man

Panacháy   My little Sister (direct address, male-speaking), often used as an endearment.

panti panti   medicinal flower, resembles a pansy

paqarin   morning

Paqarinkama!   Until tomorrow! See you tomorrow!

Pasakuy!   Go ahead! Come in!

Pasayukuy!   very polite variant of Pasakuy!

pata   place, -side, a place alongside, shore

poncho   (Spanish) A simple woven garment with a slit in the middle for the head to pass through.

puka   red

puka mama   name of a variety of potato (lit., "red mama")

puma   puma, mountain lion

puma maki   name of a variety of potato (lit., "puma paw")

punchu   same as Spanish *poncho*

P'

p'acha   clothing

p'asña   a young woman, maiden

p'ultin!   splash!

Ph (aspirated P)

phukuy   to blow; also to ritually blow the essence of something

phukuna   a metal or wooden tube about 12–18 inches long, used for blowing on the cooking fire

Q

qatay   daughter's husband or sister's husband

qatayniy   my son-in-law or my brother-in-law

qina   a flute with a notched mouthpiece

Q'

q'inku q'inku   zig-zag

q'uncha   low clay oven; cooking pots may be placed on top of it, as on a stove

R

rauk'ana   a short-handled hoe used for harvesting potatoes

riki   okay, sure, yeah
runa   an indigenous Andean person; a human being
runa ayllu   an indigenous community

S

Salud!   (Spanish) To your health!
samúwaq?   won't you rest?
Señoritáy   My little Lady (direct address; from Spanish *señorita*)
siempre   (Spanish) always
siguru   certainly, surely (from Spanish, *seguro*)
sumaq   delicious, fine
Sumaqllaña!   'Bye now!
sunqu   heart
sunqulláy!   oh my heart!
suyamúway!   wait for me!
Suzicháy   My little Susana (direct address)

T

tawa   four
tawa iskina   four corners
tayta   father
Taytalláy   My dear Father (direct address)
taytamama   parents (lit., father-mother)
Taytáy   My Father (direct address)
tira   earth, place (from Spanish, *tierra*)
Tirakuna   Sacred Places
tiyakuy   please sit down (polite imperative)
tiyayukuy   very polite variant of tiyakuy
tomakusunchis   let's drink together (polite invitation)
tomakuy   drink! (polite imperative)
tomanki   you drink
tomayukuy   very polite variant of tomakuy
tragu   cane alcohol, very cheap rum
tusuna   an instrument, or thing for dancing
tusuy   to dance

U

unkhuña   napkin-like woven cloth for carrying coca leaves and other small objects

upa   dumb; silent; shut up! (short form of upallay)
upallay   be quiet!
urpi   dove, pigeon
urpilláy   My dear little Dove (direct address), a frequently used endearment; also a casual form of thanks
ususi   daughter
Ususíy   Daughter (direct address)

V

visitamuwanki   you are visiting me here [from Spanish, *visitar*, plus Quechua suffixes -*mu* (action from periphery to center), -*wanki* (interactive, you-to-me)]

W

wakatáy   a parsley-like herb used in soup
wakcha   orphan, a person without kinsmen
wanu   fertilizer of dried animal (sheep or llama) dung
wark'a   sling
wasi   house
wayna   young
waynu   Andean song/dance form
wayqi   brother of a man
Wayqíy   My Brother; Friend, Pal (direct address, male speaking)
wiraqucha   non-runa gentleman
Wiraucháy   Sir (direct address)

Y

Yau!   (rhymes with ow!) Hey!
yawar   blood
yusulpayki   thank-you (originally from Spanish, *Dios se le pague*)

References Cited

Allen, Catherine J.

1988   *The Hold Life Has: Coca and Cultural Identity in an Andean Community.* Washington, DC: Smithsonian Institution Press.

Arguedas, José María

1978   *Deep Rivers.* Translated by Frances Horning Baraclough. Austin: University of Texas Press. Original edition, *Los Rios Profundos*, Buenos Aires: Editorial Losada, 1958.

Baker, Paul, and Michael Little, eds.

1976   *Man in the Andes: A Multidisciplinary Study of High-Altitude Quechua.* New York: Halsted Press.

Bastien, Joseph W.

1978 (reissued 1985)

Mountain of the Condor: Metaphor and Ritual in an Andean Ayllu. Prospect Heights, IL: Waveland Press.

1987   *Healers of the Andes: Kallawaya Herbalists and their Medicinal Plants.* Salt Lake City: University of Utah Press.

Bastien, Joseph W., and John M. Donahue, eds.
1981 *Health in the Andes.* American Anthropological Association Special Publication No. 12. Washington, DC.

Bateson, Gregory
1972 *Steps to an Ecology of Mind.* New York: Ballantine Books.

Bolton, Ralph, and Enrique Mayer, eds.
1977 *Andean Kinship and Marriage.* American Anthropological Association Special Publication No. 7. Washington, DC.

Brush, Stephen
1977 *Mountain, Field and Family: The Economy and Human Ecology of an Andean Village.* Philadelphia: University of Pennsylvania Press.

Cole, Peter, Gabriela Hermon, and Mario Daniel Martin, eds.
1994 *Language in the Andes.* Newark: University of Delaware Press.

Connerton, Paul
1989 *How Societies Remember.* Cambridge and New York: Cambridge University Press.

Dover, Robert, V. H., ed.
1992 *Andean Cosmologies Through Time.* Bloomington: Indiana University Press.

Flores Ochoa, Jorge
1979 *Pastoralists of the Andes.* Philadelphia: Institute for the Study of Social Issues.

Geertz, Clifford
1973 *The Interpretation of Cultures.* New York: Basic Books.

Gelles, Paul H., and Gabriela Martinez Escobar, eds. and trans.
1996 *Andean Lives: Gregorio Condori Mamani and Asunta Quispe Huamán.* Austin: University of Texas Press. Originally edited 1977 by Ricardo Valderrama Fernandez and Carmen Escalante Gutierrez, Cuzco: Centro Bartolomé de la Casas.

Gose, Peter
1994 *Deathly Waters and Hungry Mountains: Agrarian Ritual and Class Formation in an Andean Town.* Toronto, Buffalo, London: University of Toronto Press.

Gross, Daniel, ed.

1973   *Peoples and Cultures of Native South America*. New York: Natural History Press.

Harrison, Regina

1989   *Signs, Songs and Memory in the Andes: The Translation of Quechua Language and Culture*. Austin: University of Texas Press.

Higgins, Colin, and Denis Canan

1984   *The Ik*. From *The Mountain People* by Colin Turnbull, with an introduction by Colin Turnbull. Chicago: The Dramatic Publishing Company.

Isbell, Billie Jean

1978 (reissued 1985)

    To Defend Ourselves: Ecology and Ritual in an Andean Village. Prospect Heights, IL: Waveland Press.

1995   Women's Voices: Lima, 1975. In *The Dialogic Emergence of Culture*, edited by D. Tedlock and B. Mannheim, 54–74. Philadelphia: University of Pennsylvania Press.

Jackson, Robert H.

1994   *Regional Markets and Transformation in Bolivia: Cochabamba 1539–1960*. Albuquerque: University of New Mexico Press.

Klein, Herbert S.

1983   *Haciendas and Ayllus: Rural Society in the Bolivian Andes in the Eighteenth and Nineteenth Century*. Stanford: Stanford University Press.

Klein, Herbert S., Harriet E. Manelis, and Louisa R. Stark, eds.

1985   *South American Indian Languages: Retrospect and Prospect*. Austin: University of Texas Press.

Kleymeyer, Charles, ed.

1994   *Cultural Expression and Grassroots Development: Cases for Latin America and the Caribbean*. Boulder: Lynn Reinner.

MacCormack, Sabine

1991   *Religion in the Andes*. Princeton: Princeton University Press.

Mannheim, Bruce

1991 *The Language of the Inka Since the European Invasion.* Austin: University of Texas Press.

Millones, Luis, and Mary Pratt

1990 *Amor Brujo: Images and Culture of Love in the Andes.* Syracuse, NY: Maxwell School of Citizenship and Public Affairs.

Morales, Edmundo

1989 *Cocaine: White Gold Rush in Peru.* Tucson: University of Arizona Press.

Morato-Peña, Luis

1995 *Quechua Qosqo Qollaw.* Ithaca, NY: Latin American Studies Program of Cornell University.

Murra, John V.

1973 Rite and Crop in the Inka State. In *Peoples and Cultures of Native South America*, edited by D. Gross, 377–394. New York: Natural History Press.

Murra, John V., Nathan Wachtel, and Jacques Revel

1986 *Anthropological History of Andean Politics.* Cambridge and New York: Cambridge University Press.

Nash, June

1979 *We Eat the Mines and the Mines Eat Us.* New York: Columbia University Press.

Núñez del Prado, Oscar

1973 *Kuyo Chico: Applied Anthropology in an Indian Community.* Translated by Lucy Whyte Russo and Richard Russo. Chicago: University of Chicago Press.

Orlove, Benjamin S.

1977 *Alpacas, Sheep, and Men: The Wool Export Economy and Regional Society in Southern Peru.* New York: Academic Press.

Orlove, Benjamin S., and Glynn Custred, eds.

1980 *Land and Power in Latin America: Agrarian Economies and Social Processes in the Andes.* New York, London: Holmes and Meier Publishers.

Pacini, Deborah, and Christine Franquemont, eds.

1986   *Coca and Cocaine: Effects on People and Policy in Latin America*. Cambridge: Cultural Survival Report No. 23, Cultural Survival, Inc.

Poole, Deborah, ed.

1994   *Unruly Order: Violence, Power and Cultural Identity in the High Provinces of Southern Peru*. Boulder: Westview Press.

Rasnake, Roger

1988   *Domination and Cultural Resistance: Authority and Power among an Andean People*. Durham, NC: Duke University Press.

Sallnow, Michael

1987   *Pilgrims of the Andes: Regional Cults in Cuzco*. Washington, DC: Smithsonian Institution Press.

Salomon, Frank, and George L. Urioste, trans.

1991   *The Huarochiri Manuscript: A Testament of Ancient and Colonial Andean Religion*. Austin: University of Texas Press.

Schechner, Richard

1985   *Between Theater and Anthropology*. Philadelphia: University of Pennsylvania Press.

Sharon, Douglas

1978   *Wizard of the Four Winds*. New York: Free Press.

Silverblatt, Irene M.

1987   *Moon, Sun and Witches: Gender Ideology and Class in Inca and Colonial Peru*. Princeton: Princeton University Press.

Skar, Harold

1982   *The Warm Valley People: Duality and Land Reform Among the Quechua Indians of Highland Peru*. Oslo: Oslo Studies in Social Anthropology 2, Universitetsforlaget. Distributed by Columbia University Press, New York.

Smith, Gavin A.

1989   *Livelihood and Resistance: Peasants and the Politics of Land in Peru*. Berkeley: University of California Press.

Soto-Ruíz, Clodoaldo

1993   *Quechua, manual de enseñanza*. Lima, Peru and
           Urbana-Champaign, IL: Instituto de Estudios Peruanos
           and Center for Latin American Studies, University of
           Illinois.

Spalding, Karen

1984   *Huarochiri: An Andean Society under Inca and Spanish
           Rule*. Stanford: Stanford University Press.

Starn, Orin, Carlos Ivan DeGregori, and Robin Kirk, eds.

1995   *The Peru Reader: History, Culture, Politics*. Durham and
           London: Duke University Press.

Tedlock, Dennis

1995   Interpretation, Participation, and the Role of Narrative in
           Dialogic Anthropology. In *The Dialogic Emergence of
           Culture*, edited by D. Tedlock and B. Mannheim,
           253–288. Urbana and Chicago: University of Illinois
           Press.

Turnbull, Colin

1972   *The Mountain People*. New York: Simon & Schuster.

1979   Anthropology and Drama: the Human Perspective. In
           Anthropology, Drama and the Human Experience,
           edited by Colin Turnbull and Nathan Garner, 1–14.
           Washington, DC: The George Washington University.

Urton, Gary

1981   *At the Crossroads of the Earth and the Sky: An Andean
           Cosmology*. Austin: University of Texas Press.

Van den Berghe, Pierre

1977   *Inequality in the Peruvian Andes: Class and Ethnicity in
           Cuzco*. Columbia: University of Missouri Press.

Weismantel, Mary

1988   *Food, Gender and Poverty in the Ecuadorean Andes*.
           Philadelphia: University of Pennsylvania Press.

Whitten, Norman, ed.

1981   *Cultural Transformation and Ethnicity in Modern
           Ecuador*. Urbana: University of Illinois Press.

Wright, Ronald, with Nilda Callañaupa

1989   *Quechua Phrasebook*. Hawthorn, Victoria, Australia: Lonely Planet Publications (P.O. Box 2001A, Berkeley, CA 94702).

FILMS

Cohen, John

1984   *Mountain Music of Peru*. Berkeley: University of California Extension Media Center.

1991   *Carnival in Q'eros*. Berkeley: University of California Extension Media Center.

1992   *Dancing with the Incas*. Berkeley: University of California Extension Media Center.

Getzels, Peter, Harriet Gordon, and Penelope Harvey

1990   *The Condor and the Bull*. NFTS, Station Road, Beaconsfield, Bucks, Great Britain, HP9 ILG.

NOVA Series

1993   *Shadow of the Condor*. Boston: WGBH TV

Yule, Peter, and Andy Harris

1987   *Our God the Condor*. New York: Filmmaker's Library.